THE CARDINAL ALLEN
GRAMMAR SCHOOL

AWARDED

to

MAURICE PHILLIPS

FORM 1 JOHNSON

1976–7

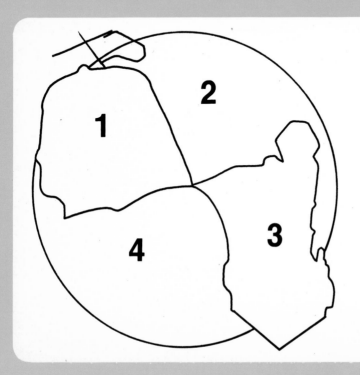

KEY TO COVER

1. Trans-European Express

2. Locomotive at Jenbach, Austria

3. An early American express locomotive

4. A British freightliner train

An early signalman *(spine)*
Richard Trevithick's locomotive, 1804 *(back)*

Purnell's FIND OUT ABOUT

TRAINS
and RAILWAYS

Purnell's FIND OUT ABOUT
TRAINS
and RAILWAYS

Artists

Jim Bamber
Paul Bernson
Annie Calloway
Ray Calloway
Dick Eastland
Gerry Embleton
Phillip Emms
Dan Escott
John Hoffer
Illustra
Eric Jewell Associates
Mike Kelly
Brian Lubrani
Peter North
Barry Salter
Bob Scott
Michael Trimm
Gary Walser

Written by: Bill Gunston

Contributor: Stephanie Thompson

Editorial: Anne-Marie Ehrlich
Keith Faulkner
Peter Luff
Graham Marks
Trisha Pike
Martin Schultz

Produced by Theorem Publishing Ltd., 71-73 Great Portland St., London,
W1N 5DH for Purnell Books

Published 1977 by Purnell Books,
Berkshire House, Queen St., Maidenhead
Copyright © 1977 Purnell and Sons Limited

SBN 361 03884 4

Made and printed in Great Britain by Purnell & Sons Ltd.,
Paulton (Bristol) and London

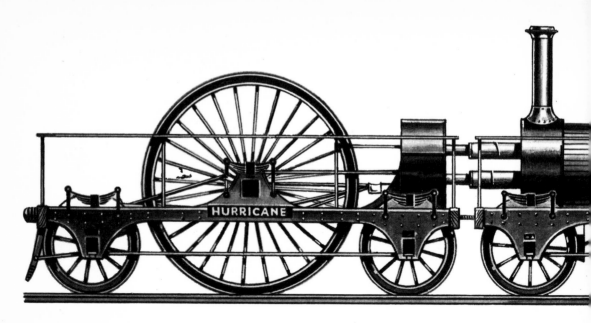

CONTENTS

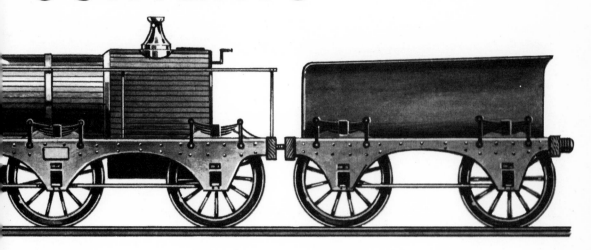

FAMOUS ENGINES

The earliest railway engines were among the first machines that ever moved about by mechanical means. They emerged from inventors' backyard sheds snorting and chuffing, and belching smoke and steam. Nothing like them had ever been seen before. Gradually, improvements were made. Engines grew in size and power. Locomotives were given a cab to shelter the crew and some, like the Dominion of Canada, shown below, were built to a streamlined design.

Trevithick's Engines

Richard Trevithick was one of Britain's first great engineers. In 1799 he built a small steam-driven car which he chuffed merrily along the streets and up the hills of Cornwall. His second vehicle was exhibited in London and, in 1803, he built a steam locomotive to run the 15-kilometre railway of an ironworks in South Wales. This became known as the famous Pen-y-Darran railway.

Many industrial railways already existed, but the trucks were hauled by horses (you can read about horse-drawn trains on pages 140 and 141). Some people laughed at Trevithick's steam engine, but the Pen-y-Darran ironmaster, Samuel Homfray, bet a rival that the locomotive would be able to haul ten tonnes of iron along the route. The rival took the bet, which was for 500 guineas (£525), as much as most men then earned in a lifetime.

There was great excitement as Trevithick finished the engine, lit the fire and tested it. Hundreds of other bets were placed as people gambled on the Pen-y-Darran engine. Then came the great day, on 21 February 1804. The snorting engine easily hauled not only the ten

Above: *Pen-y-Darran, Richard Trevithick's famous engine which, in 1804, successfully won a wager by pulling ten tonnes of iron along a 15-kilometre route in Wales that everyone except Trevithick said would be impossible.* **Right:** *The small circular track built at Euston in London where Trevithick's second engine, Catch-me-who-can entertained the crowds.*

tonnes, but also 70 cheering passengers who were thrilled at being the world's first passengers in a train. The journey took four hours, but this was because the train had to stop every few hundred metres while overhanging branches were cut and rocks were removed from the line. But though it won the bet, this engine was too heavy for the flimsy track, and it never went into regular use.

So Trevithick next built Catch-me-who-can, a lighter engine which, in 1808, went into regular service carrying passengers round a small circular track near what is today Euston Road in London. This was only a form of entertainment, but the speedy little engine (which Trevithick unsuccessfully tried to run against a racehorse) was the world's first ever to pull fare-paying passengers.

Above: *Richard Trevithick, one of Britain's first engineers.*

Puffing Billy

The main lesson of the Pen-y-Darran locomotive was that steam engines need strong rails, or the track will break up under their weight. Many of the early railways did not really have 'rails' at all, but instead thin plates, which is why men who look after track are still called 'platelayers'. But by 1810 engineers were busy designing strong rails for steam engines and, in the following year, an engine built by Matthew Murray and John Blenkinsop went into regular use at a coalmine in Yorkshire, England. The original line had been built in 1758, but new rails were put down, one of which had a 'rack' of projections sticking out sideways to engage with the teeth of the driving wheel of the engine. Another change was that two cylinders were used, instead of one.

But William Hedley, of Wylam coalmine in northern England, was sure the engineer (named Blenkinsop) was making a mistake with his complicated toothed drive. He decided to get his own engineer, Christopher Blackett, to build some locomotives with plain, smooth driving wheels. The result was a series of engines that were famous ever afterwards, with the names Puffing Billy, Wylam Dilly, and Lady Mary.

Left: *Puffing Billy was the first of a long line of famous engines which ran on smooth driving wheels.*

Though often derailed by bad track, which would not carry their great weight of about eight tonnes each, they worked well for more than 50 years and were several times rebuilt to make them work even better. All had two cylinders outside the boiler. These fine engines, dating from 1813-15, proved that the smooth-wheeled engine could work.

Above: *A view of Puffing Billy in the Science Museum of London. Puffing Billy was built in 1815 and it lasted for many years.*

Stockton & Darlington

One of the first people ever to grow up with railways was George Stephenson, born at Wylam in 1781. In 1812, he was made **enginewright** of the local coalmine where, from 1814, he built a succession of engines each better than the last. One of his first big improvements was to redesign the driving system. A little later he overcame the noisy blasting hiss that had given Puffing Billy its name. Instead of just letting the used steam escape out of

Below: *Locomotion No. 1 was the first steam locomotive to run on a public railway. Weighing 6½ tonnes, it had the 0-4-0 wheel arrangement, and is believed to be the first engine ever built with outside coupling rods linking the driving wheels. The wood-slatted boiler had a very small working pressure and the tractive effort (pull) was just 453 kilos.*

the cylinders, he drove it into the funnel. This helped to silence the engine and also make it work more powerfully.

In 1822, Stephenson was appointed engineer to a completely new railway linking the important city of Darlington with the port of Stockton. It was the first public railway in the world to use steam locomotives and also the first to use the new iron rails. These rails were laid on stone blocks with no **sleepers** joining them, so it was a very suitable route for horse-drawn traffic. But Stephenson managed to persuade the Stockton & Darlington Railway to buy a steam engine so as to draw trains fitted in between the horse traffic. The result was Locomotion No. 1, and it stole the show at the opening ceremonies of 27 September 1825.

Though at first a man on horseback led the way waving a red flag (because there were such crowds that officials feared an accident), Locomotion proved itself the best engine yet, pulling 38 coal wagons, each weighing three tonnes, with 600 people sitting on top!

One of the odd features about Locomotion was that its wheels were made of inner and outer parts fixed together by stout, wooden **pegs**. A big advance was that front and rear wheels were made to go round together by connecting rods projecting from both wheels on each side.

The train, with a total load of 90 tonnes, travelled at about 70 kph. Its success caught the imagination of people all over the world.

Above: *George Stephenson was one of the first and greatest of the engineers of the Industrial Revolution. Entirely self-taught, he became both famous and very rich.*

Stephenson's Rocket

Several successful engines were built by different designers during the 1820s, but their great chance came in 1830 when plans were drawn up for a new railway to link two of Britain's greatest cities, Liverpool and Manchester. This was by far the most important railway at the time and it was the first in the world planned to use mechanical **traction** for every train.

Most engines were now following an accepted design. They had a boiler with a **safety-valve** in case steam was made too quickly, a firebox, smoke-box and chimney, two cylinders and wheels. Dry steam collected in the dome above the boiler. From there it went along a pipe to the cylinders where valves controlled the quantity of steam entering and leaving. The **tender** contained coke for the fire and water for the boiler.

George Stephenson was appointed the railway's engineer, but it was his son Robert who did most of the work designing and building the Rocket, the most famous railway engine in history. It was really not quite as good as some earlier designs. With only two driving wheels and cylinders very awkwardly angled, the whole engine tended to wobble violently from side to side and up and down when it was pulling a heavy load. But it was also a simpler and more straightforward engine.

The Rocket weighed only five tonnes, but easily hauled 13-tonne trains at the then amazing speed of 24 kph. When it was run at full power, it went at almost twice the speed. Painted yellow, this neat little engine seemed just like a rocket. During the Rainhill Trials, held to choose the best engine for the new railway, the Rocket impressed everyone with its speed and simple design, and easily came first.

Not only did the Rocket win the trials, and the big prize of £500, but it made certain that the Liverpool & Manchester Railway would have its trains hauled by steam engines. The new line was opened by the Duke of Wellington on 15 September 1830, the first public railway to be run entirely by locomotives. It was the beginning of the railway age.

Right: *The Rocket was probably the most famous railway engine in history. Though it was by far the fastest vehicle then made by man, its main technical advance was that it had a boiler filled with tubes carrying the hot gases from the fire to the chimney. But the Planet (inset) was even better.*

The First Americans

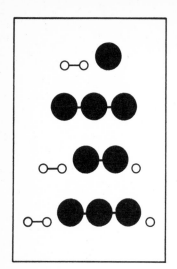

The first locomotive to run in North America was not particularly famous; it was named the Stourbridge Lion and was delivered by a British firm in 1829 to work for the Delaware and Hudson Canal Company. Much better known was the American-built Best Friend of Charleston, which went into use on the South Carolina Railroad in 1830, only three months after the opening of the Liverpool & Manchester Railway in Britain. This line in the United States grew swiftly until, in 1833, it reached 978 kilometres, at that time the longest track in the world.

The extraordinary thing about Best Friend was its big upright boiler which looked like a bottle. It was wood-fired and the engine worked well, but in 1831 a tragedy occurred. A foolish enthusiast riding on the **footplate**

Above: *Wheel arrangements of steam locomotives grew more complex over the years. The 4-2-0 (top) is seen in the illustration on this page. Goods engines often had the 0-6-0 form, with just three coupled axles. The two lower types are the 4-4-2 Atlantic and 4-6-2 Pacific.*

Below: *The Experiment rode the track better, because of its pivoted bogie at the front. It was built in 1832.*

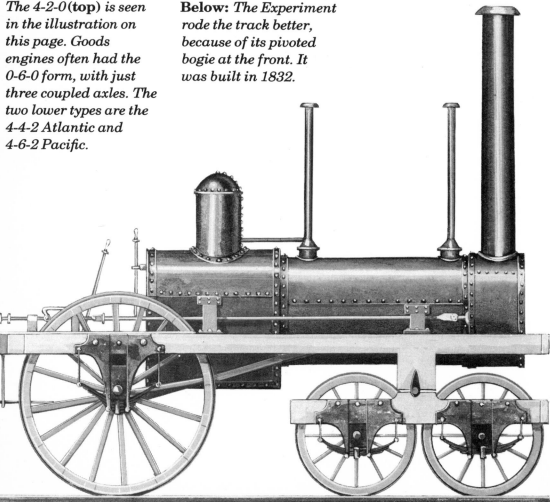

Above: *The Best Friend of Charleston went into action for the first time on Christmas Day, 1830. It worked well until the boiler blew up because someone—probably not the fireman but a passenger riding on the engine—tried to get more steam pressure by closing the safety-valve.*

(this is the floor of the locomotive) tried to make the engine go faster by pulling down on the boiler safety-valve to prevent it from blowing-off steam as the pressure inside rose. Eventually, the Best Friend exploded in a cloud of scalding steam.

More important in railway history were the Experiment and Washington. The Experiment was the first locomotive to have a **bogie**, a four-wheel truck with a joint to enable it to pivot, to help it run round bends in the line. Earlier British engines had caused difficulty with the rough American track, but this new engine with its swivelling bogie rode beautifully. It was also the fastest vehicle ever made by man at that time, being able to keep up a speed of 96 kph. This was the magic 'mile a minute'.

The Washington was built a little later and was important in setting the fashion that lasted more than half a century and made nearly all American engines look alike: A 4-4-0 (four-wheel bogie, four driving wheels and no trailing wheels), she had a **cow-catcher** in front, a huge **smokestack** and enclosed cab.

In winter, a huge **headlamp** was necessary to light up large obstacles like snow-laden trees. Sometimes the light track collapsed under the extra weight of snow, or cracked in the severe frost, and forest fires were a constant hazard.

Borsig of Berlin

So great was Britain's leadership with railway engines that even mighty Germany bought nearly all its earliest locomotives from British builders. A few were also imported from the United States, and one of the best

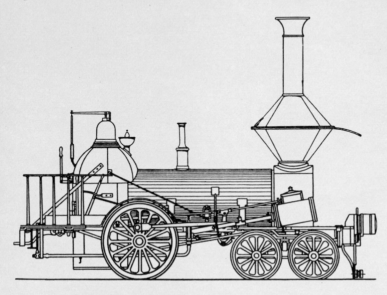

designs appeared to be that of William Norris of Philadelphia, whose 4-2-0 wheel arrangement provided a very efficient running performance.

A man who was to become one of the greatest European locomotive builders, Herr A. Borsig of Berlin, chose the Norris 4-2-0 as the basis for his first engine, Borsig No. 1 of 1841. He added an extra trailing wheel under the footplate where the driver (engineer) and fireman (stoker) worked, making his engine a 4-2-2. Though a fine-looking engine, the extra **axle** took a lot of weight off the driving wheels. The Borsig engine was one of the first of thousands of steam locomotives which were to have great difficulty getting in motion without the wheels slipping on the smooth rail and spinning round uselessly.

Borsig learned his lesson, however, and in 1844 he sold the Berlin-Anhalt Railway an engine in which the extra trailing wheels were connected to the driving wheels to make a 2-4-0. This wheel arrangement was later used for many hundreds of successful Borsig engines sold in many countries. His works also constructed large numbers of 2-2-2 engines, which differed in details but (unless the customer specially asked for something different) always came painted deep green,

Right: *By the 1840s railway locomotive designers were in business all over Europe and in North America. One of the more successful designs is the German engine dating from the 1850s. Built by Borsig of Berlin, it had the luxury of a cab to shelter the crew from the weather.*

Below: *Borsig's first locomotive was built in 1841. Its design was inspired by the American engines designed by Norris, one of which (**left**) was bought by the Berlin-Potsdam Railway in 1839. The fantastic funnel was designed to trap sparks when burning wood, which was the most common fuel in America.*

with a brightly polished brass dome on the boiler. The Germans called these engines 'Spinat mit Ei', meaning spinach with egg!

Much later, in 1935, Borsig's works built what was probably the biggest steam passenger engine in Europe. It was a monster 4-6-4, with driving wheels 2.2 metres in **diameter**, and covered in a streamlined casing. It was built for speed, and it set a speed of 200 kph, a world record. (You can read about this on pages 28 and 29.)

The Crampton

Thomas Russell Crampton was a bright young locomotive engineer in Britain. He was one of the first men to grow up as an employee of a big railway; he served on the Great Western, the most advanced line in the world (you can read about this on pages 54 and 55). He soon began to sketch engines of his own. He was certain that he could design an engine which could be used for the ordinary kind of railway, with the rails laid to a **gauge** (distance between the rails) of 1.5 metres, that was just as powerful and as fast as those used on the 'broad gauge' of two metres used on the Great Western. Nobody seemed to be interested, however, but in 1845 he succeeded in building such an engine. It was to become one of the most widely used engines in Europe.

The chief feature of his engine was a single pair of huge driving wheels placed right at the back, like the paddlewheel of an old Mississippi riverboat. In front

Below: *Throughout the mid-19th century the Crampton was a type of engine seen all over Europe. A few worked on British railways such as the London & North Western, but most served on the Continent.* **Bottom:** *The photograph shows a Crampton of 1863.*

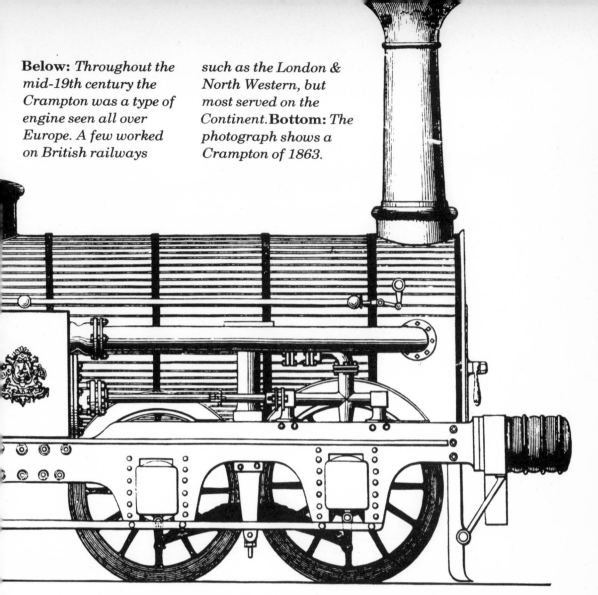

were either two or three pairs of fixed front wheels (not a bogie). This long and rigid arrangement, with the big driving wheels and **cranks**, made Crampton engines hard on the track, and they were not used much in Britain. But in Europe they became so important that 'prendre le Crampton' (take the Crampton) was the common way of saying one was going on a long journey. One good point about these engines was that they were extremely easy to maintain, whereas with some locomotives it took many hours of work to make even the simplest repairs.

The first Cramptons, for Belgium and Scotland, were built in 1847. Some were being made 30 years later, and at least two are still in existence. To show what these engines could do with light trains, in 1855 one averaged 100 kph all the way from Paris to Marseilles on the French coast.

Mud-diggers and Camels

The need to pull heavier trains brought about a big change in the appearance of engines. Light passenger trains could be pulled at high speed by engines such as the Crampton, with a single pair of large driving wheels. Each **revolution** of these wheels made the train go further, so high speeds were easy to attain. But heavy goods trains did not need speed, and so the driving wheels could be made smaller. Halving the size of the driving wheels doubled the **tractive effort** (the amount of energy needed to pull the train). To stop such wheels from slipping, it was necessary to increase the weight pressing them down on the rail, but this would mean that the wheel and rail would wear out quickly and might even break, as the old plate rails had done. The answer was to use a lot of small driving wheels, coupled together.

By 1843, Ross Winans in the United States had designed an 0-8-0 **freight** engine. Not only did it have terrific tractive effort, but the whole weight of the engine was on the driving wheels, so slipping was avoided. In 1844, Winans began delivering twelve to the great 'B & O', the Baltimore & Ohio Railroad, where they became known as 'mud-diggers' because they churned up the ground under the track.

Winans was also responsible for designing the famous 'camel' engines. They were called this because the cab-driver sat high up, on top of the boiler, rather like an Arab traveller on top of a camel's hump (you can read about this engine on pages 130 and 131). The 'camels'

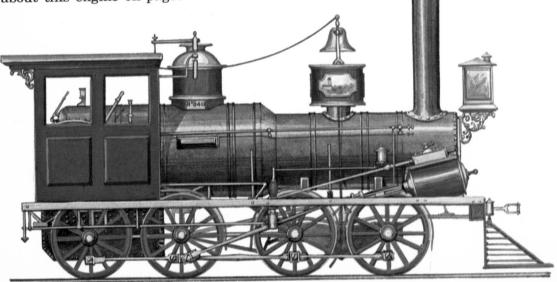

Above: *The Mud-diggers, built by Ross Winans in the U.S.A., were some of the world's earliest freight engines, with many small driving wheels. Such engines were well suited to pulling heavy logging trains over hastily laid track to the sawmill.* **Left:** *This fine eight-coupled freight locomotive was one of the early products of the Baldwin works.*

were very powerful engines and also extremely economical to run (their use of fuel was quite low for their performance) and Winans built about 200 of these engines altogether.

Below: *Union Pacific 4-8-8-4 Big Boy. As more and more goods began to be transported across America on the railroad, freight trains increased in size.*

The Super Pacifics

Sir Nigel Gresley was one of the most famous railway-engine designers in history. He worked at Doncaster, the Yorkshire engine centre of the Great Northern Railway. In 1922, Gresley produced the first of his super-express passenger engines, the Flying Scotsman. They bore the same name as the train they pulled, because that was the name of a famous racehorse, and all the first 110 Gresley engines were named after winners of the Derby horse-race. They were bigger and more powerful than other British express engines, having the 4-6-2 wheel arrangement which by that time had become known as the Pacific layout. With six coupled wheels, the boiler could be made longer to give more steam and pull heavier trains.

In 1934, a Gresley Pacific pulled the Flying Scots-

man train at over 160 kph, and the following year another, named Papyrus, reached 173 kph. By this time, Gresley was building the successor, the A4 class, with driving wheels of two metres diameter, three big cylinders and a boiler working at a very much higher pressure. Gresley wanted these more powerful engines for a new and very fast train of special coaches, which, like the engines, were streamlined, and painted silver-grey. On 27 September 1935, the new train, called Silver Jubilee, and pulled by the first A4, named Silver Link, steamed out of London filled with special guests. The run was fantastic. The train averaged an amazing 148 kph all the way.

Gresley made many of the superb A4 engines. Later ones, even better than Silver Link, were painted blue and named after birds. On 3 July 1938, one of these engines, Mallard, was driven at full throttle down the long slope on the way to the central British city of Peterborough. It reached 202 kph with a seven-coach train, setting a world record for steam traction that still stands today.

Left: *Specially built for speed, this monster Borsig 4-6-4 set a steam record at 200.4 kph in 1936. Two years later this was just beaten by Britain's Mallard* (**right**), *a famous Gresley Pacific.*

Left: *One of the classic steam classes, a Gresley Flying Scotsman type Pacific, at full speed with a Scottish express.*

Streamlined for Speed

Faced with the terrific competition of the new diesel locomotives in the 1930s, American steam-locomotive designers hit back with the best and most powerful engines the United States had ever seen to try to keep steam alive in North America. The Big Boy was the greatest of the steam freight locomotives. Passenger engines were often almost as large, but they had bigger driving wheels and had to combine high tractive effort with great speed. None were more perfectly typical of the great American express engines than the beautifully streamlined and very elegant Hiawatha classes of the 1930s.

The Hiawatha was actually a train, running from Chicago through Milwaukee to St. Paul/Minneapolis, a very fast route without severe slopes. To fight off competition from cars and buses, and increasingly from the airlines, the Chicago, Milwaukee & St. Paul Railroad improved the tracks and the trains, and instead of going

Above: *The British Southern Railway's last steam engines (Tangmere is pictured) had their streamlining later removed.*

Above: *One of the few drawbacks to streamlining steam locomotives was that the added casing made maintenance more difficult. To get at the smoke-box of the Princess Coronation British engines, large doors had to be opened in the front of the casing.*

Below: *To haul the crack Hiawatha express the Milwaukee Railroad used the biggest (236 tonnes) 4-4-2 engines ever built.*

over to the diesel like **rival** railroads, it decided to electrify some lines and build better steam engines for the rest.

To pull the speeded-up Hiawatha train, the company built the finest 4-4-2 Atlantic locomotives ever designed. This wheel arrangement was a copy of that used at the turn of the century, but in fact it was perfectly suitable for these engines of 1936. The need was not so much for great tractive pull; it was for speed, and the American 4-4-2 engines that pulled the Hiawatha regularly ran faster than any steam locomotives had ever done before. They were actually extremely powerful, and compared with the European Atlantic locomotives they were gigantic.

The Hiawatha trains were the last, biggest and fastest with this wheel arrangement ever constructed, and they were a complete success. Dead on time, they would take the Hiawatha at 160 kph with less fuss, less noise and less wind disturbance than earlier engines had caused when running much slower. Finally, in 1938, the railroad brought in even bigger streamlined 4-6-4 (Hudson wheel arrangement) engines. This was to enable the locomotive to keep up the same speed with heavier trains.

Steam Goliaths

Below: *The Union Pacific Big Boy class were the greatest steam engines of all time. A fleet of 25 worked gigantic freight trains, weighing up to 13,000 tonnes, from the Rocky Mountains to the Pacific. Despite their colossal bulk, they often travelled at speeds as high as 96 kph, and could develop well over 6,000 horsepower. One of these monsters, No. 4012, is preserved in working order at Steamtown, a great American railroad museum in Vermont.*

From about 1850 onwards, British locomotives tended to be smooth and pretty, and they had to be small to fit the loading gauge (the maximum width and height allowed on the railway). The American engines, on the other hand, were designed not for prettiness but for hard work, and they could be made bigger. There were fewer obstructions, the tunnels were larger, and the rails were heavier and stronger. So engines in the U.S.A. grew larger and larger. Soon they were too long to go round bends, and the Mallet arrangement (you can read about the Mallet on pages 136 and 137) was adopted to make what was really two engines supplied by one gigantic boiler. They pulled the heaviest trains in the world.

Biggest of all were the so-called Big Boys class, built for the Union Pacific Railroad from 1941, right at the end of the life of steam engines in America. They were huge freight engines, but very successful and well-liked. Their wheel arrangement was 4-8-8-4, and their huge boilers supplied steam to four cylinders far bigger than anything ever used in Europe. The firebox had a **grate area** of almost 14 square metres, bigger than the floor of an average living room, and it was fed with coal by a mechanical stoking system at the rate of about 23 tonnes per hour. Water was pumped into the boiler at twice this rate. The engine alone weighed 346 tonnes. Coupled on the back was the tender carrying coal and water which brought the total weight up to nearly 540 tonnes.

FAMOUS TRAINS

A key feature of nearly all the special named trains has always been comfort. When an American introduced a very comfortable coach 100 years ago, called a Pullman after him, some railways made up special trains composed entirely of such coaches and named the train a Pullman. American trains led the way with special kinds of passenger car, such as club cars, parlour cars, and barber shops. Today, trans-continental trains are even fitted with vistadomes, such as in the photograph below.

Across the United States

America, the land of private **enterprise**, naturally built a wide variety of quite different, privately owned railroads. However, with incredible foresight, they almost all agreed to use the same rail gauge as 'the old country' (Britain) of 1.5 metres, so trains from one line could run on the rails of another. Competition, however, was as sharp as a razor, and **rival** lines soon tried to out-do each other in putting on trains that were faster or more luxurious. Unlike Europe, the American coaches hardly ever had any class distinction. Even today there

Right: The No. 999 was probably the most famous locomotive in American railroad history. One of the last and greatest of the classic 4-4-0 engines, it hauled many of the crack 'limited' expresses of the New York Central, and, on 10 May 1893, is reputed to have touched 180 kph near Batavia, NY.
Left: Some 45 years later the same trains were being hauled by 4-6-4 engines which weighed 260 tonnes with their 140-tonne tenders. They regularly worked the 1,000-tonne Twentieth Century Limited at 128 kph.

are still many railway systems in Europe where travellers have a choice of greater or lesser luxury, at higher or lower fares. Some countries even had four classes in each train! In the United States, this was thought unpleasant, and the railroad simply made the whole train as comfortable as possible, though some did offer special coaches at higher fares.

The most important long-distance route was New York to Chicago, linking the top two cities of the nation. The whole north-eastern U.S.A. soon became a dense **network** of lines, and the traveller had a wide choice of routes between the two cities. But in 1902, the very important New York Central & Hudson River Railroad

attempted to capture the bulk of the traffic with a super-express called the Twentieth Century Limited.

This was a time when many U.S. trains were being called 'limiteds', so-named because the number of tickets sold was limited to the number of seats. This was not easy to arrange, because tickets could be bought at many different stations, each of which had to know how many seats were left on each train. The new express ran over the flat 'water-level route' up the Hudson to Albany, across New York state to Syracuse, Rochester and Buffalo, across Pennsylvania to Cleveland, Ohio, and finally across Indiana and round the south shore of Lake Michigan to Chicago.

In 1905, the rival Pennsylvania Railroad fought back with the Pennsylvania Limited, which ran faster over the shorter but more hilly route from Jersey City, only 1,452 kilometres instead of 1,576. The Pennsylvania special took only 18 hours for the whole run at a very good average of over 80 kph.

Left: *The Empire State Express in 1952 pulled by a diesel locomotive. By the 1950s diesel power as a means of haulage was spreading rapidly throughout the North American rail system.*

37

Great European Expresses

Perhaps the most famous train in history was the Orient Express. It has provided the setting for many novels and films (in one the whole action takes place aboard this train), and was supposed to carry **diplomats**, spies and other exciting passengers. Certainly it was the most international train imaginable, because from 1883 it went right across Europe, from Paris to the city that used to be called Constantinople (now called Istanbul) in Turkey. On the way it called at such important cities as Strasbourg, Munich, Salzburg, Vienna, Budapest (today the capital of Hungary), Belgrade (today the capital of Yugoslavia) and Sofia (now the capital of Bulgaria). The same train went the whole way, taking 81½ hours, and a

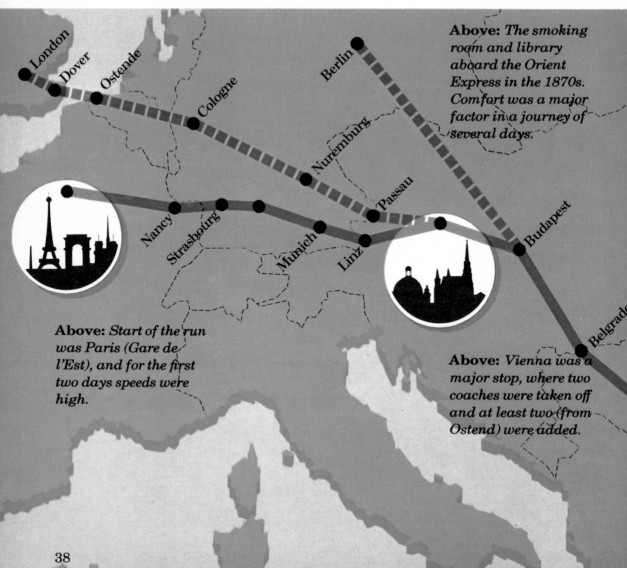

Above: *The smoking room and library aboard the Orient Express in the 1870s. Comfort was a major factor in a journey of several days.*

Above: *Start of the run was Paris (Gare de l'Est), and for the first two days speeds were high.*

Above: *Vienna was a major stop, where two coaches were taken off and at least two (from Ostend) were added.*

passenger could make the whole journey in the same seat or lying in the same bed. Different locomotives and crews from the national railway systems pulled the train across each country.

France had many famous trains running from Paris to the sunny Mediterranean. The best known of all was the Train Bleu (the Blue Train). It was a heavy train of **luxurious** cars all painted a rich blue. This ran on the PLM (the Paris, Lyons, Mediterranee) line. Of course, nearly everyone who used it was going on holiday, and the train was very luxurious, with comfortable armchairs that could be moved about, superb service and the best food and wines in the restaurant car. In the old days some families hired complete coaches. After the Second World War the National French Railways replaced this historic train with a completely new one called Le Mistral.

Below right: *In the course of its great run of 2,800 kilometres, the Orient Express ran over the metals of many railways, hauled by perhaps eight or nine different types of locomotive. But the same coaches covered the whole journey.*

Sofia

Left: *Destination was Constantinople, today called Istanbul.*

Longest Railway in the World

The longest railway journey in the world is that from Moscow to Vladivostok, a single main line stretching 9,303 kilometres. When it was built, between 1891 and 1899, it was called 'a rusty streak of iron through the vastness of nothing to the extremity of nowhere', but that was a rather dull description. Since then it has become a mighty transport system running through a gigantic land of vast, untapped wealth. At the same time, everyone knows that the climate in Siberia is the harshest in the **inhabited** world, with winter temperatures down to minus 50°C. Building and operating the

Above: *In old Imperial Russia, on Sundays, a church-coach was attached at the rear.*

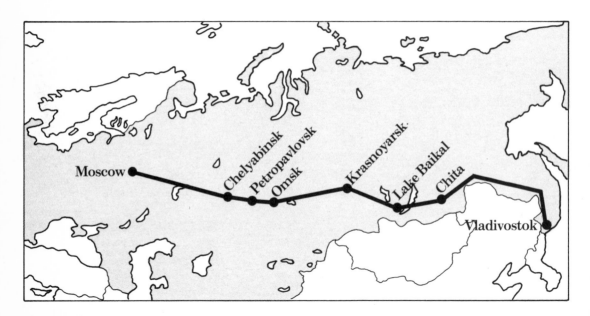

Trans-Siberian Railway was very difficult.

The Trans-Siberian Express began operating the complete 9,303-kilometre route in 1905. At first, it took two weeks to make the trip, but even this was good in the circumstances. Passengers had time to get to know each other, and they would get off and buy food at the various stops. In winter, there were log or coke fires in the coaches, two baths, a piano, a gymnasium, and in the corridors were urns of hot water for making tea. On Sundays, before the 1917 **revolution**, a car equipped as a church was hitched on the back. Sometimes the train would stop for quite a long period while the passengers helped the train crew gather firewood. Over the western sections the engine would be a coal-burner.

When the Russian **engineers** reached mighty Lake

Above: *Route-map of the longest railway journey in the world. The total distance from Moscow to Vladivostok is 9,303 kilometres by rail, a journey made longer by the need to steer well clear of China. Major improvements have included the line round Lake Baikal, and electrification of the route.*

Baikal, just north of the Mongolian border, they had to build a train ferry to carry the trains to the far shore. The great lake is more than 1.6 kilometres deep, the deepest in the world, and round the shore were steep mountains. But the train ferry could not break through the ice in winter. So the Russians laid tracks on the ice, but in the spring the ice cracked and a locomotive sank. Eventually, the railway was carved out of the mountainside all round the south shore for 400 kilometres, one of the greatest feats ever of railway engineering. Today, the whole route is double-tracked, and nearly all **electrified**. In 1960, the 5,200 kilometres from Moscow to Irkutsk was electrified, the longest electric route in the world, and trains now do the whole journey in just seven days.

Below: *Contrasts in the Trans-Siberia over a period of 50 years. The small picture was taken in 1911, and shows that often two steam locomotives were needed to haul the assemblage of freight and passenger cars. The larger illustration, taken near Lake Baikal, shows one of the powerful electric locomotives now used.*

Golden Arrow

Before the air age, travellers who wanted to go from Britain to Europe (Britain did not then regard itself as being part of Europe), had to catch a train in London. They could then either stay on the train and cross the Channel or North Sea on a train ferry, or leave the train, take a fast boat to a foreign port and then catch a **Continental** train from there. The system worked well, and was extremely important (imagine what it would be like if all the air routes to Europe suddenly stopped). Of course, each trip meant travelling on at least two different railways.

In 1926, the Nord (Northern) Railway of France began running a special luxurious all-Pullman express from Paris to Calais, where its passengers joined the cross-Channel steamer. The express was named Fleche d'Or (Golden Arrow), though it was not really coloured gold; the engine was brown and the coaches were the brown and yellow that always marked them as Pullmans. After three years, a further improvement took place. The British Southern Railway introduced its own all-Pullman Golden Arrow and the two railways worked together to arrange the quickest total time between the centres of London and Paris. A special fast ship, Canterbury, was built to carry passengers between Calais and Dover. The trains carried special signs on the front, complete with a large golden arrow.

This train is one of the few long-established named expresses that still runs. Today, it is all-electric. In some international trains **customs officers** ride on the train to save travellers' time, but this has never been done with the Golden Arrow. The train would have become unnecessary if the Channel tunnel had been built. It would then have been possible to run expresses straight through at full speed between the two capitals.

Below: *The Golden Arrow (in French, the Fleche d'Or) is one of the few survivors of the famous old named expresses that still runs. Today it is hauled by electric locomotives, in both Britain and France, but until about 1965 the British Rail Southern Region used these fine 4-6-2 steam locomotives. Originally, they were streamlined, but to make it simpler to look after them they were de-streamlined as shown in this picture of engine 35015 Rotterdam Lloyd leaving London.*

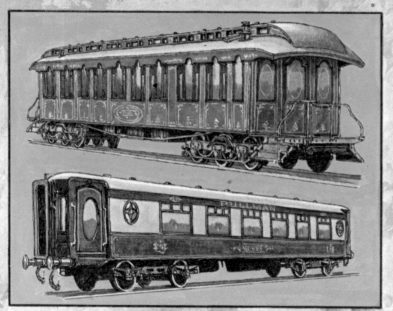

Left: *The vision of George Mortimer Pullman of America led to the most comfortable passenger coaches of their day, not only in his native America but also across Europe (where they were often run by the Wagons-Lits company). The upper coach is one of the first Pullmans of 1880. Below is a British car of the 1945-60 era.*

Speed in Germany

In the 19th century, Germany was made up of lots of small kingdoms and dukedoms such as Saxony, Bavaria, the Palatinate and Wurttemburg and each had its own railway. But when these were made into German State Railways, the brilliant German engineers began setting speed records and running some of the best trains in Europe. As early as October 1903 a Siemens electric railcar set world speed records at 199, 205 and finally 210 kph and, in June 1931, another railcar driven by a **diesel** engine and airship **propeller** reached 230 kph. This was

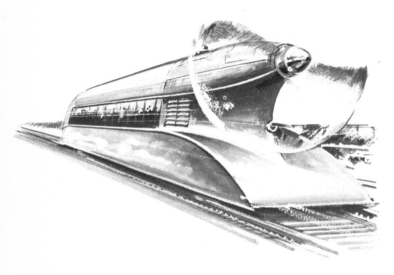

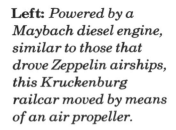

Left: *Powered by a Maybach diesel engine, similar to those that drove Zeppelin airships, this Kruckenburg railcar moved by means of an air propeller.*

not a regular train, but another German development soon set the highest regular rail speed in the world. The Fliegende Hamburger (Flying Hamburger) was a diesel two-coach train which from 1932 averaged 124.5 kph.

This train was powered by Maybach diesel engines, but the Germans also set a world speed record with a steam locomotive. It was probably the biggest and most powerful express engine ever made in Europe, and it had 4-6-4 wheel arrangement, with driving wheels no less than 2.2 metres in diameter. Its huge boiler worked at the high pressure of 128 kilograms per square centimetre. Called just '05.001', it went out with a test train in early 1935 and set a speed of 210 kph.

The most famous express of the old Bavarian State Railways was called Das Rheingold (after **legendary** gold reputed to be stored by Rhinemaidens), and its coaches belonged to the Mitropa Company, the German equivalent of Pullmans. Today, the train still runs, pulled at 160 kph by an electric locomotive. It is now one

Left: *The Fliegende Hamburger (Flying Hamburger) was the fastest regular scheduled train in the 1930s. Usually a two-car unit, with Maybach diesel engines, it ran on German State Railways from 1932.*

Below: *Pride of the modern DB (Deutsche Bundesbahn, German Railways), the Rheingold was originally a steam express but today is a TEE (Trans-Europe Express) electric train.*

of the luxurious Trans-Europe Express (TEE) trains (you can read about this express on pages 178 and 179). So is Das Rembrandt, named after a famous painter, which runs from Amsterdam in Holland to Mannheim in Germany and then divides, one part going to Zurich in Switzerland and the other speeding on to Munich. In modern Europe, fast expresses are no longer held up at frontiers, but can link city centres in about the same total time that it takes to go by jet.

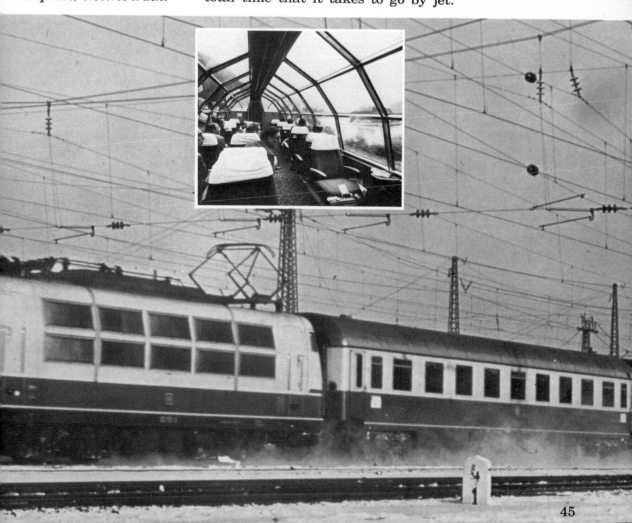

Diesel Streamliners

By 1930, three-quarters of all Americans who made journeys by public transport went by train. But at the same time the number of passengers was falling. Americans were changing to the car, the Greyhound bus, and the new airlines. The old trains seemed doomed to die. But the managers of many railroads saw a way to present a new image, and at the same time make trains go much faster and need fewer stops. This was to use diesel-electric power, build much lighter trains, and cover them in streamlined casings painted in bright colours.

First to do this was the mighty Union Pacific, which in 1933 began running a train called City of Salina (after a town in Kansas). It had three cars, linked by **bogies** joining **adjacent** cars, and weighed the same as a single old-fashioned Pullman coach. It was comfortable, the **exhaust** was much less bothersome than steam and smoke, and it could average 144 kph, and reach speeds up to 176 kph. Many people thought of it not as a train, but rather as a kind of bus on rails. But in 1934, the very similar Burlington Zephyr, with three stainless-steel coaches riding on a total of four bogies, ran the 1,600 kilometres from Denver to Chicago non-stop, a world record. It did the journey in 14 hours, at the fantastic average of 124.8 kph, and really made people take notice. Later that year the Union Pacific streamliner averaged 165 kph over a stretch of 90 kilometres. The Rock Island line began running its Rockets, and the Illinois Central

Above: *One of the first and most famous of the American streamliners in the new diesel era was the Super Chief, of the Atchison, Topeka & Santa Fe Railroad. Here it is seen leaving Chicago in 1952, by which time it had grown to need a four-unit diesel-electric locomotive, with a total horsepower of 7,200.*

46

Left: *By 1952 the Burlington Zephyr had new coaches with vistadome cars to give passengers an all-round view. This picture shows the rear end of the Zephyr as it speeds through Aurora, in Illinois.*

put on the Green Diamond in May 1936, linking Chicago and St. Louis.

Then came really big diesel streamliners, with separate multi-unit locomotives pulling long and heavy trains. First came the Super Chief of the Atchison, Topeka and Santa Fe, with two 1,800-**horsepower** diesel-electric engines (you can read about diesel-electrics on pages 88 and 89), which ran non-stop from Chicago to Los Angeles in 39 hours. The City of Los Angeles and City of San Francisco of the Union Pacific were even bigger, with a three-unit 5,400-horsepower locomotive and 15-car train including barber shops and **vistadomes**. All these were in use before 1937, completely changing the face of the American railroad, and sweeping away the steam locomotive.

Below: *This is how the Burlington Zephyr looked in 1934, as it raced 1,600 kilometres non-stop at extremely high speeds. Such trains helped to meet the competition of airlines.*

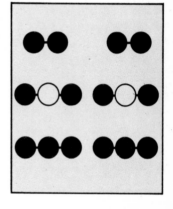

Above: *Diesel and electric locomotives have a different scheme of wheel arrangement, with driving wheels lettered and other wheels numbered: top, BB, middle, A1A-A1A, bottom, CC.*

Le Mistral

The SNCF, French Railways, suffered terrible damage during the Second World War. After 1945, it was rebuilt very quickly and made far better than ever before. On the great main line from the Gare de Lyon (Lyon's station) in Paris, southwards through Dijon, Lyon, Marseilles and the Côte d'Azur (the French Riviera holiday coast on the Mediterranean), the old PLM track was completely rebuilt, **realigned** and electrified. The SNCF decided to supply electric current at 1,500 volts through a cable running along above the trains, instead of through extra rails. It is difficult to use extra electrified rails at over 1,000 volts, whereas with fully **insulated** overhead cables the voltage can be as high as 25,000.

To run the new electrified line, the SNCF built locomotives of tremendous power. Some were called BB types, with four-wheeled bogies (electric and diesel

Left: *Track can be electrified in various ways. Long routes usually have an overhead wire, called a catenary, as seen in the picture above, but lines in cities have a third rail. The current rail may be in the centre* (**far left**) *or close on the outside of a running rail.*

engines used A for single axles, B for pairs, C for three-wheeled bogie and so on) and the bigger ones were CC, with six-wheeled bogies. All could develop more than 5,000 horsepower, and some give over 8,000. In 1955, the SNCF did special high-speed trials on another electrified line south of Bordeaux. One BB, with a three-car train, reached 330.6 kph, shattering all previous world rail-speed records. The next day a CC did the same speed. These records have never been broken.

With the powerful new electrics the SNCF set up a system of great expresses that have established a wonderful record of high speed, long-distance running, and keeping to **schedule** to the minute. The most famous train of all is the reborn Mistral, named after the fast hot

Above: *The Mistral express of the SNCF (French Railways) is one of the biggest and fastest passenger trains in the world. It was steamhauled at first (below, at Nice with giant 2-8-2 on the front), but after 1950 the line was electrified at 1,500 volts.*

wind that often blows from the south into France. Though it weighs 1,000 tonnes, this great and luxurious train averages 128 kph from Paris to the Mediterranean. On the same route runs the Blue Train and the Flanders-Riviera Express. On the route from Paris to Toulouse, Le Capitole is timed to run between Les Aubrais and Vierzon, 70 kilometres apart, at 201 kph.

In 1955, the French National Railways arranged a special high-speed test run that took over a year to prepare. Two specially-constructed, three-car trains, geared for high speed, raced along a track at 330 kph. This record has not yet been beaten by a train on normal tracks.

Below: *The Mistral in 1955, hauled by a type of BB that once reached 330 kph.*

D

Above: *A guard of the London & Birmingham (later London & North Western), in 1832-52.*

Left: *Early railways, such as the Festiniog line of 1836, adopted impressive crests and badges, but by the 1930s this changed to simpler symbols, called logos, such as that of the GWR (left) and British Rail (below).*

Famous Insignia

All the old railway companies designed for themselves what modern **advertisement** experts would call 'an image'. Like the horse stagecoaches, they painted their passenger coaches in gay and distinctive colours and, after a while, they did the same with the engines. In Britain, it was thought best for each of the many companies to have distinctive engines and coaches; for example, the Great Western had coaches dark brown below and cream above, hauled by dark-green engines with distinctive polished brass steam domes and a polished copper band round the funnel. A dull sameness of colour could be found only in the United States and Canada for a while, with coaches all of natural wood, hauled by engines painted black. But in today's stream-lined diesel and electric age, North American trains have become a blaze of colour, and each line has done its best to impress its 'image' on the public.

The old railways had badges and coats of arms. These were complicated, and made little impact on the public beyond giving the impression that the line was

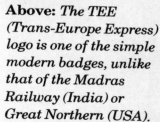

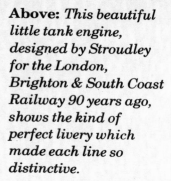

Above: *This beautiful little tank engine, designed by Stroudley for the London, Brighton & South Coast Railway 90 years ago, shows the kind of perfect livery which made each line so distinctive.*

Above: *The TEE (Trans-Europe Express) logo is one of the simple modern badges, unlike that of the Madras Railway (India) or Great Northern (USA).*

reliable and trustworthy. Many of the railways around the world, both in the vast British Empire and in many completely foreign countries, were built by British engineers and often owned by British **shareholders**. They therefore often had Union Jacks in their crests or coats of arms. Some of these badges are still used today, though in many cases the railway now has nothing to do with Britain (most had to be sold to help pay for the Second World War). Even in Britain and other European countries, nearly all the proud old railways have vanished, swallowed up into great **nationalized** rail systems. Partly for this reason, the old coats of arms and other mementoes are eagerly collected by **enthusiasts** who love the old railways.

Today's **insignia** are quite different. They are never ornate and complicated and do not try to look like the coats of arms of high-born families. Instead, each one is simple and bold, and is intended to have an impact on the public. The name of such modern symbols is a logo. It is seen on trains, stations, railway road vehicles, notepaper, advertisements, timetables, posters and everywhere else the railway can get publicity.

THE MEN WHO BUILT THEM

After 1830, Britain, which led the world in the railway revolution, went through a form of 'railway mania'. Everyone who had any money tried to invest in the railway and many grew rich from it. But other people tried to stop the coming of the railways. Landowners sent their men to prevent the surveyors from planning the route. But most people welcomed the railways, and out in all weathers armies of navvies could be seen building the railways—except at Kilsby, below, where they were deep in a tunnel.

Brunel the Master-builder

Isambard Kingdom Brunel was one of the most famous engineers in all history. Born in 1806, he began to work under his father M. I. (later Sir Marc) Brunel in 1823. Two years later he started the Thames tunnel, and the picture shows him explaining progress to his father (who is wearing the top hat). He later built the famous Royal Albert Bridge near Plymouth.

Right: *Brunel's greatest achievement was the Great Western Railway (GWR). He was appointed chief engineer of the new line when he was 27, and he worked day and night planning the great railway from London to Bristol, designing bridges and tunnels.*
Below: *He even spent days at a time out on his horse surveying the countryside.*

Above: *One of the greatest tasks in building the GWR main line was tunnelling through a great hill near Box, east of Bath. Box Tunnel remains today a giant memorial to Brunel's artistry.* **Right:** *Bristol Temple Meads station was the original terminus of the GWR, and is still in existence.*

Left: *One of his last achievements was the colossal Great Eastern, launched in 1858 and far bigger than any other ship for the next 40 years. But the worry of this ship wore him out, and he was also worn down by the fight to try to preserve the broad gauge of the GWR. He lost the fight, not because the 143.5 cm gauge was better, but because the narrower gauge had been chosen by all his rivals.*

Giants of the Early Railways

It was inevitable that the railway mania should have brought to the fore a few great railway men; men who became skilled and trusted leaders either of railway construction or of building engines and rolling stock. Perhaps the greatest name of all was that of Stephenson. George Stephenson and his son Robert were unquestionably the greatest designers of locomotives in the first half of the 19th century. Even the great Brunel had purchased some very bad engines, and did not get reliable trains until he bought Stephenson engines (the North Star, one of Robert Stephenson's first for the Great Western, is still in existence). Robert was appointed sole **engineer** for the mighty London and Birmingham Railway, by far the biggest and most difficult railway **enterprise** of the whole period before 1850 (you can read about this on pages 76 and 77). He was especially noted for his bridges, which included the unique Britannia Bridge across the Menai Straits from Wales to Anglesey.

Building the railways was by far the biggest constructional job ever undertaken in the history of the world, far more extensive than the Great Wall of China or the Pyramids. It needed tens of thousands of tough men, the navvies (you can read about the navvies on pages 58 and 59), and these men had to be organized. In Britain, one of the greatest railway builders was George Hudson. He saw how silly it was to build hundreds of small railway companies, each linking just two or three towns or villages, and his efforts to form bigger railways made him one of the first men to be called a **financial tycoon.** His biggest achievement was to make many small lines into the great Midland Railway, which was efficient, cheap and profitable. Eventually it was found he was sometimes so determined to win that he broke the law, but it was largely through him that by 1850 Britain had 9,650 kilometres of efficiently run railways.

Another great pioneer was Thomas Brassey, who built railways all over the world. In 1835, he had to build part of the Grand Junction line, and then found himself employing 3,000 men and managing **contracts** worth over four million pounds sterling (a fantastic sum 140 years ago) building the London & Southampton line. Eventually, he had an army of navvies numbering 75,000, in nine European countries, as well as Canada, India, Africa, South America and Australia.

Above: *Thomas Brassey (1805-70) was the greatest builder of railways in the world. He employed an army of up to 75,000 men working in as many as nine countries at once, on every continent.*

Above: *The Britannia Bridge across the Menai Straits was built in 1849. It is unique.*

Right: *In the quarter-century 1825-50, hundreds of railways were built throughout Britain. At first there were too many small ones, but after 1850 they began to merge. This was the map in 1850.*

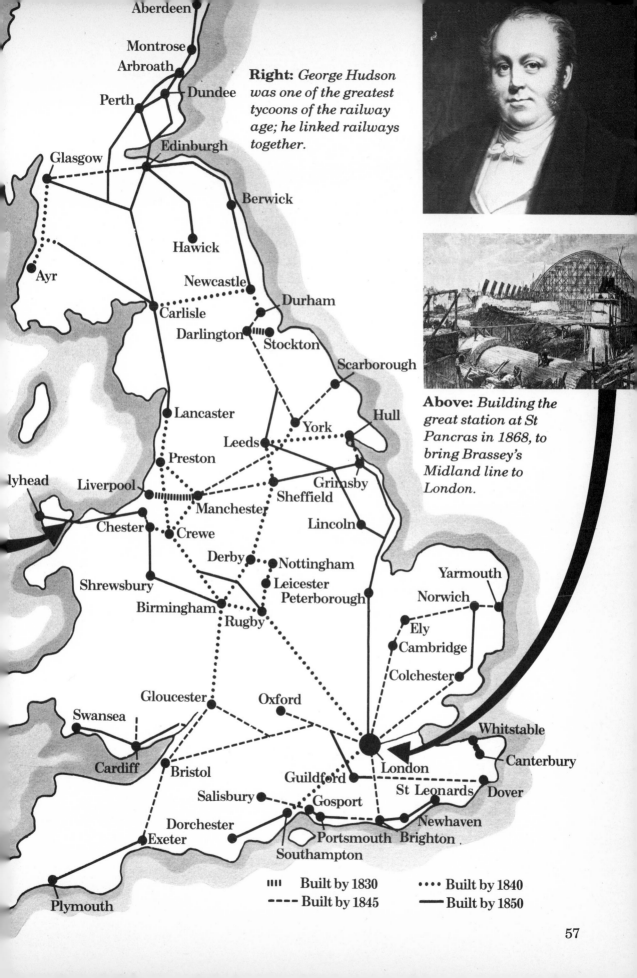

Aberdeen

Montrose

Arbroath

Perth

Dundee

Edinburgh

Glasgow

Berwick

Hawick

Ayr

Newcastle

Carlisle

Durham

Darlington

Stockton

Scarborough

Lancaster

Hull

York

Leeds

Preston

Grimsby

lyhead

Liverpool

Sheffield

Manchester

Lincoln

Chester

Crewe

Derby

Nottingham

Shrewsbury

Leicester

Birmingham

Peterborough

Rugby

Yarmouth

Norwich

Ely

Cambridge

Colchester

Gloucester

Oxford

Swansea

Whitstable

Cardiff

Bristol

Guildford

London

Canterbury

Salisbury

St Leonards

Dover

Dorchester

Gosport

Exeter

Portsmouth

Brighton

Newhaven

Southampton

Plymouth

Right: *George Hudson was one of the greatest tycoons of the railway age; he linked railways together.*

Above: *Building the great station at St Pancras in 1868, to bring Brassey's Midland line to London.*

| IIII | Built by 1830 | •••• | Built by 1840 |
| --- | Built by 1845 | --- | Built by 1850 |

The Navvies

When the British canals were built, the labourers who dug them were called navigators, shortened to navvies. To build the railways thousands of these men were needed, because there were far more railways and they were built more quickly. By 1846 the number of navvies in Britain had reached 200,000, and by 1850 there were over a million in the whole world. They were tough men, and lived in a world of violence and high spirits. They were well-paid for the times, often getting as much as five shillings a day; and each day, with nothing but hand tools and barrows, they could move 20 tonnes of soil. They lived in dirty camps of tents and shacks that moved along with the building of the line. But they ate huge amounts of the best steaks and got drunk almost every night.

Most of the navvies were employed by specially formed big rail construction companies, such as Brassey's, Cubitt's and Peto's (the first big civil engineering firms in history). They wore heavy clothes, often of corduroy, with a stout hat and non-slip sandals. Their gear included a pick, shovel, wheelbarrow, lantern and, usually, a sword and a clay pipe. A large number were Irish, and almost all of them loved fighting. They got their fill of this whenever **rival** lines struggled to build to the same town. Sometimes they fought pitched battles, one of the most famous being the 'Battle of Havant' in 1858, when the London, Brighton & South Coast railway tried to stop the London & South Western from building their line to Portsmouth.

In Britain, the vast hordes of navvies were feared and hated by the respectable people because of their wild lawlessness. In fact, the way they lived was natural, and

they deserve great credit for doing a fantastic job. There was very little real injury or bad feeling as a result of their battles, but this was not the case with the vicious competition between American railroad builders. Thousands of navvies there, who mostly came from the railways of Britain and Europe, often became involved in bloody wars. Bridges were weakened so that they collapsed, locomotives were used as battering rams to charge through **barricades,** guns were fired, and men killed. Only gradually did the U.S. railroads learn to live together.

Below: *The navvies were a great army of individualists, tough, wild and undisciplined but capable of working hard in all weathers. Their toil on the railways changed the world.*

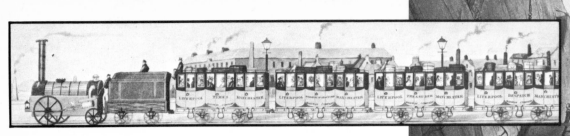

Liverpool to Manchester

As the world's first all-steam public passenger railway, the Liverpool & Manchester had to do many things for the first time. Even in its original construction a large number of problems had to be solved. Though the two cities are only 48 kilometres apart, from the station in Liverpool to that at Water Street, Manchester, the line was very hard to build. From Crown Street the line climbed very steeply through a tunnel to Edge Hill. Tunnels had been dug for canals, but sloping railway tunnels caused new difficulties. The track would have to pass under a great Moorish Arch, a difficult task.

Just beyond the Moorish Arch the line would have had to climb over Olive Mount. Instead, Stephenson boldly cut right through, running the tracks along the bottom of the steep-sided Olive Mount cutting. No canal had ever been dug through solid rock with such a deep cutting with almost **vertical** walls. We can imagine how tricky the work must have been, with navvies clinging to the walls with fingers and toes as they broke the rock with picks and lowered the large bits with cranes.

Nearer Manchester was a quite different kind of problem. Chat Moss was a vast marsh across which it was said no man could ever go. Stephenson had to overcome **superstitious** people who said the trains would vanish in the 'bottomless' bog, never to be seen again. But he put in drainage, and carried the track on deep piles, and the dreaded Moss was conquered. This was just the first of many ways in which railways gradually changed the face of the world.

Top: *A first-class passenger train on the newly opened L & M line, with a Royal Mail coach and a private horse-carriage.* **Right:** *A goods train pulled by the North Star. Passengers could ride on the freight.*

Above: *The greatest day in the history of world transport up to that time was the opening of the L & M railway on 15 September 1830. The picture above shows the scene at the Moorish Arch. Just beyond this vast ornament the track was laid through a hill in Olive Mount Cutting (left). This deep cutting, with almost vertical sides, was one of the most difficult civil-engineering feats men had ever attempted.*

Spanning a Continent

Throughout history, the size of a country tended to be roughly limited by how far a man could ride a horse in a day, from a capital near the centre. Europe thus became covered with small countries which, because of old agreements or natural features such as rivers or mountain ranges, often had very irregular shapes. For the first time, the U.S.A. was planned as a gigantic country made up of states which, except for the states in the north-east, were bigger than European countries, and shaped regularly with straight borders. This was possible mainly because of the railways. With railways, a much bigger nation could be held together by fast **communications**. The trans-continental American railroad was the first of the giant rail-routes spanning the continents over distances measured not in tens of kilometres but in tens of thousands of kilometres.

In the mid-19th century, most of the United States was rough, lawless and sparsely inhabited. Many of the Indian tribes were dangerous and killed **surveyors** and

Right: *The Golden Spike was a traditional ceremony at the completion of a new railroad in North America. The rails were pinned down by spikes of steel, but the very last spike needed to finish the line was made of gold, and this was driven home by the chairman of the line. This illustration represents the occasion when the Union Pacific*

met the Central Pacific. Two special spikes were driven, one of silver and the other of gold. The teams of navvies were delighted and celebrated with hard liquor. This was thought improper by many Americans, who had an official picture painted with no bottles visible, and the navvies replaced by elegant gentlemen and ladies.

engineers trying to prepare the way for the line. There were also rival American rail companies, which often battled with each other for rights to land.

Then, in 1862, at the height of the bloody Civil War (the first war in which trains were important, and you can read about it on pages 156 and 157), the vast job of linking the Atlantic and Pacific was undertaken in earnest. Tens of thousands of labourers, mostly Chinese, toiled eastwards from San Francisco with the Central Pacific. Daily they pushed four or five kilometres towards the Rockies, laying the heavy rails on timber ties (sleepers) and securing them not with bolted 'chairs', as in Europe, but with long spikes driven in by sledgehammers. In the mid-west, pushing westwards from Omaha, toiled thousands of navvies, mostly Irishmen fresh from European rail construction. The two teams met, amidst noisy rejoicing, at Promontory Point, Utah, on 10 May, 1869. The last two spikes were driven: one of Comstock silver and the other of California gold. The great railroad was complete.

Tunnelling Through the Alps

Railways can cross mountains by **spiralling** up along the slopes, and special railways can be built able to climb steep mountainsides (you can read about this on pages 132 and 133). The first railway across a mountain range was built in 1854 at Semmering in Austria, where a competition was held to choose the best locomotive to pull trains up the steep **gradients.** But no train in the world could climb the steepest gradients on the Alps, which lie right in the heart of Europe. They were a barrier to trains between France, Switzerland, Germany, Austria, and Italy until, in 1871, the Mont Cenis tunnel was opened, allowing trains to run from France to Turin and northern Italy. The 13-kilometre tunnel had taken 13 years to cut, using picks and shovels. A temporary track was laid over the pass to carry workers and the **spoil** they dug out, but it was wrecked by **avalanches.** Inside the great tunnel men were killed, and ventilation was

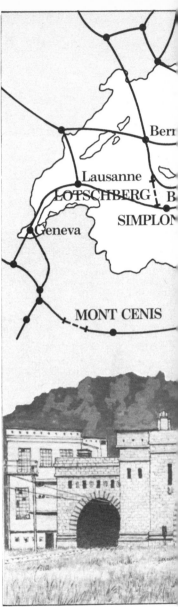

Left: *When it was being built at the turn of the century, the Simplon Tunnel was the most difficult engineering task men had ever attempted. This photograph was taken in 1899, in front of the southern portal in Italy. They were among the last of the navvies who gave the world its network of railways.*

difficult. Unlike tunnels through ordinary hills, it was impossible to put down a number of **shafts**: the Alpine tunnels had to be made as two dead-ends, which had to meet in the centre.

In June 1872, work began on a bigger tunnel, the St. Gotthard, between Göschenen and Airolo in Switzerland. It was 14 kilometres long, with double tracks. Favre, the engineer in charge, died at his job inside the tunnel in July 1879. Not until 29 February 1880 did the two groups of tunnellers meet. A **ballast** train ran through on Christmas Eve 1881, and the tunnel was opened on 27 May 1882. It was the longest in the world until an even longer and deeper tunnel was opened on 1 June 1906 after seven years of toil. By this time, explosive blasting and hydraulic drills were in use, and the hollow drill cutters wore down from 60 to 7.5 centimetres in biting through the hard rock. As many as 300 cutters were used up in a single day. The 20-kilometre Simplon tunnel was backed up in 1922 by a slightly longer second tunnel right alongside.

Above: *Though a small country, Switzerland is packed with railway wonders. The map shows some of the great tunnels through the Alps, and immediately below, a train, headed by a Swiss CC locomotive, is seen leaving the Simplon tunnel.* **Right:** *Tunnelling was hard and dangerous.*

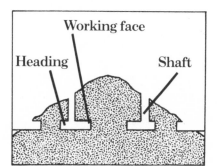

Working face

Heading

Shaft

Left: *Tunnels through ordinary hills could be built by first sinking shafts and headings. With the immensely high Alpine mountains tunnels were constructed by digging them from either end.*

The Tay Bridge Disaster

Most of the disasters happened on railways in newly opened-up places, where conditions were wild and tough. In Britain, the land where railways grew up, accidents became unusual because of good engineering and discipline. But there was one terrific disaster which, though it did not claim a very great number of lives, was of a kind that set people talking for months. Had it happened 50 years earlier, it would have seemed to support those who said railways were wicked and the work of the devil, and might have prevented railways from ever being built.

The Tay, the longest river in Scotland, reaches the North Sea in a broad **estuary** three kilometres across. For many years this was much too wide for a bridge, and trains from the south had to make a long **detour** through Perth, or else passengers got off and crossed to the city of Dundee by a ferry. But the North British Railway built a great bridge in the mid-1870s, far longer than any previously attempted. It struck straight out across the cold grey waters, with the rails carried far above on tall steel columns standing on solid concrete foundations. It was opened in 1877, and in 1878 Queen Victoria rode across the wonderful bridge. But it contained fatal flaws. The columns were strong vertically, but were not designed to resist heavy loads from the sides; and in many places the steel plates and **rivets** were dangerously cracked or weakened.

On 28 December 1879, Scotland was hit by a storm, with gales more violent than anyone could remember. As darkness fell, the mail train from Edinburgh rumbled onto the great bridge, heading north for its destination, Dundee. It never arrived. Not until next day did horrified rescuers find that the whole middle of the mighty bridge had been blown over sideways, carrying the engine crew and 78 passengers to their deaths. But there was no reason why a properly built bridge should not have survived the gales, and in 1887 the railway opened the new Tay Bridge, 19 metres upstream of the old one, and a little more than three kilometres long. It has stood firm ever since.

Conquering Nature

Below: Railroads made travel easier for everyone. Before this great viaduct was built travellers in this region of the Rockies had to clamber down the slope of a mountain and then, after crossing a valley where there was no road, climb up another slope on the other side. It was the same all over the world.

Throughout the 19th century thousands of kilometres of new railway were built almost every year. When all was added together, this represented by far the biggest single job ever done by humans. In fact, it was easily the greatest of man's attempts to overcome the barriers of nature and provide a link between existing cities and land where new cities could be built. In Europe, the railways made communications easier and swifter between established cities, but elsewhere it was the railway, more than anything else, that opened up millions of square kilometres of land to settlement and exploitation.

Above: *Starting the first train to run in China. The place was Shanghai, 1876, at the opening of the Woosung line to Kungwang.*

Above: *Two British-built engines toil up a steep slope with a train from Colombo to Kandy, Ceylon (now Sri Lanka). This was 1876.*

The hundreds of thousands of kilometres of railway built in 1830-1930 crossed arid deserts, steaming jungles and icy mountains. They were built by people of every race and creed, though usually led by Europeans, who lived in their hundreds of thousands in tents, shacks, bunkhouses or specially built bunk cars which rolled along on the freshly laid metals.

Always the line was built against time. Sometimes this was so that the railway could earn money more quickly for the people who had paid for it to be built. Sometimes it was to beat a rival line that was striving to reach the same city. Sometimes it was even a matter of national politics. For example, after 1880 the Americans were pushing ahead with the Great Northern north-west from Chicago to Seattle, and the British feared that if they beat the Canadian Pacific the Americans might take over British Columbia. Hurriedly, the Canadian line was built. It was made to cross hundreds of gorges and ravines on hastily built timber trestles, sometimes with a sheer drop of several hundred metres.

In India, timber trestles were eaten by white ants, causing trains to crash. Rivers flooded, washing tracks away. Avalanches swept rails and trains down mountainsides. The railway builders kept discovering new problems and finding fresh solutions, and the railways kept growing.

RAILWAYS CHANGE THE WORLD

Probably man's first transport 'system' was by water—along the rivers and over the seas. However, this system was only useful to people who lived on river banks and sea shores. About 300 years ago men tried to bring water transport to more people by building canals. Then the railways came and slashed the cost of carrying goods, and for the first time in history rich and poor alike could undertake long journeys and push back the limits of their world. As you can see in the photograph below railways now do the work of the waterways.

The Rainhill Trials

When the Liverpool & Manchester Railway was being planned, between 1826 and 1829, the directors were uncertain how the trains should be pulled. They were generally agreed that steam power was better than horses, but knew about the problems of the early engines. Often these broke down, or just worked badly, and their weight sometimes broke the rails. With fast passenger trains (something that the L & M planned to introduce for the first time), broken rails would be very dangerous. So some directors said the best method of pulling the trains was big steam engines in **stationary** houses. Here winding ropes on drums would pull the trains up to the drum, where the rope from the next winding house would take over. But George Stephenson, who was a powerful man in an argument, said this was nonsense. He would build engines to run along the track, pulling fast trains without breaking down or destroying the rails.

To settle the matter, the directors organized a great

Above: *Though today almost forgotten, Timothy Hackworth's Sans Pareil (no equal) was possibly the best engine in the Rainhill trials. Unlike the Rocket it had four coupled wheels, and Hackworth thought he had a better boiler with the exhaust steam making a blast up the chimney to draw air through the fire (as done in every steam locomotive since).*

Left: *Another of the losers was the original favourite of the crowds, Novelty. Though neat and capable of exciting sprints at up to 64 kph, Novelty kept going wrong.*

contest. They offered a prize of 500 pounds sterling for the best locomotive that could run up and down a stretch of their new railway at Rainhill, just east of Liverpool, for 112 kilometres without giving trouble. Very strict conditions were laid down, the chief technical ones being that the locomotive had to pull a 20-tonne train at 16 kph, and must not itself weigh more than six tonnes on six wheels or four and a half tonnes on four wheels.

To make sure that nothing would go wrong, very complete details were worked out as to the performance required. To avoid any possibility of confusion, it was decided that each locomotive should be tested on a separate day.

Eventually, most entrants never got their engines ready, and the Sans Pareil was disqualified by failing on its eighth return trip. After putting up some wonderful fast runs, Ericsson's Novelty had to be disqualified because its air bellows kept going wrong and she never completed a single series of runs. This saddened the crowd because the quiet and graceful Novelty had been the hot favourite. The clear winner was Rocket, by George and Robert Stephenson, which met all the conditions. Neat and fast, she reached 46 kph, and weighed four and a half tonnes. She was sold to the railway for 500 pounds, and Stephenson engines were bought to work the other L & M trains.

Trains and Cities

One of the conditions laid down in the Rainhill trials had been that 'engines should effectively consume their own smoke'. In 1829, nearly all people lived in what we would today call the country. Cities were generally small (though crowded) and the problem of industrial **pollution** had, until then, hardly been noticed at all.

The new rule about smoke, however, shows that the L & M directors were eager that their railway should be popular, and that the scared members of Parliament and other critics, who said steam locomotives were devilish things that would destroy the pleasant countryside,

Above: *In the mid-19th century, the new steam locomotives came into sharp conflict with traditional transport. Here in Philadelphia, U.S.A., men with flags had to be present to prevent possible collisions or other sorts of accident.*

Below: *By 1870, London had the Metropolitan Railway running below its streets.*

should be proved wrong. Smoking engines in the country were not much of a problem, but in the city centres it was another matter. Here the smoke problem was made worse by the fact that many engines might be in a station at once. The fact that the railway would probably be in a deep cutting or have several underground tunnels, which are obvious smoke traps, would only tend to make matters worse.

Some cities, such as Cambridge, refused to let the railway come near. Then the city council reluctantly let the Great Eastern build a station, provided it was right

Above: *Dating from 1863, this painting shows Baker Street station on the Metropolitan.*

outside the city and had only one platform! In other cities, the fact that there were so many rival rail companies led to the construction of two, three, four or even more separate stations. Nobody knew how a station should look; some lines built miniature castles or palaces, while St. Pancras in London was called St. Pancras' cathedral. In 1863 came a totally new development: the Metropolitan Railway, in London. This was the first railway intended to run wholly within one city, to ease the **congestion** in the streets. At first it was a choking underground tunnel full of smoke, but before long electric trains were running. Today almost all **urban** 'one-city' railways are electric. Compared with the electric underground railways of the past, the modern underground system is remarkable. These railways cause a great deal less noise and pollution than the traffic on the roads.

Right: *The Royal Albert Bridge was Brunel's last great railway job. It carried the GWR across the Tamar from Devon into Cornwall in 1859.*

Left: *The Landwasser (land-water) viaduct is one of the many spectacular engineering feats of the Rhaetian railway in Switzerland. Trains cross the valley and go straight into the face of a mountain.*

Right: *Typical of the ornate engineering of the Victorian era is the turreted facade of Clayton tunnel, on the main line of the London, Brighton & South Coast railway. Built like a medieval castle, it is still in use, but today with the line electrified.*

Under and Over

Ordinary trains could not travel up and down steep hillsides. Sometimes the track was made to climb steep slopes by means of spirals, or a switchback arrangement (which meant the trains had to keep stopping and reversing). More often, hills were cut through by a cutting or tunnel, while deep valleys and river gorges were crossed by a bridge or viaduct (a long bridge over a sunken stretch of land). These were among the most difficult parts of the early railways to build. As the Tay Bridge disaster showed (you can read about this on pages 66 and 67), even after 1870 people still did not quite know how to make strong steel bridges, though stone and brick viaducts had been built by the Romans.

The first major railway bridge, made of iron, was over Gaunless Valley, on a branch of the British Stockton & Darlington line to Bishop Auckland. Built by

George Stephenson between 1824 and 1825, it worked well but had to be replaced when trains became heavier. Other famous early bridges included the Britannia Bridge built by Robert Stephenson over the Menai Straits between 1846 and 1850, in the form of a long square tube; Brunel's great Royal Albert Bridge (you can read about this bridge on pages 54 and 55); and the Forth Bridge, opened in 1890, which is so large it takes three years to paint, and as soon as they have finished, the painters always have to start again! The first great viaduct was on the London & Greenwich line, opened in 1838, but a much bigger viaduct is at Morlaix in France.

Early tunnels were smaller than the ones through the Alps (you can read about the tunnels through the Alps on pages 64 and 65), but they were difficult enough to build. When Robert Stephenson was building the London & Birmingham Railway in the mid-1830s, the great tunnel at Kilsby, near Rugby, nearly defeated the whole project. The broad hill was water-sodden quicksand, and time after time the tunnel either collapsed or was flooded. It cost about a million pounds, and many lives, to drive the tunnel through and make it safe.

Above: *Built like a Roman aqueduct, this fantastic viaduct was built between 1846 and 1851. It lies on what is today German State railways at Gölzschthal, between Reichenbach and Plauen.*

Decline of the Canals

When the railways were being built, nearly everyone, from 1830 onward, welcomed them. They meant profits, easier travel, a higher standard of living, extra jobs, quicker deliveries and lower prices. But a few people did not think the railways were a good thing. The first people who were against the railways were traditional country people, set in their ways, who simply could not come to terms with any change that was so big and noticeable. Another enemy was the landowner, who just did not like having railway track run across his property. But before long there were many who had a better reason to dislike the new form of transport.

Chief of the enemies were the old carters, bargees and ferrymen. The carters were the workers, often self-employed, who carried goods and sometimes people on lumbering carts, with broad wheels to stop them sinking

Left: *Today most of Britain's canals are sleepy and deserted, except for holidaymakers. They long ago lost their place as the leading trade arteries of the nation to the railways. Yet until the 20th century they were still very important. The big picture (**below**) shows the Midland railway crossing a canal in the 1890s. The scene is wintry, and though the ice did affect the railways it had a far worse effect on the canals, and often caused them to freeze up entirely.*

into the mud roads. They soon realized that they had no chance of competing with the trains, and if a new railway was built on one of their routes they had to find customers somewhere else. It led to cut-throat competition between the remaining carters, and to fights and disputes; and if the carters could hurt the railway they would. As for the canal bargees, they fared even worse. They had seldom carried passengers, but the whole **commerce** of the nation had depended on the canals in the early 19th century. Now the steam trains were moving goods quicker and cheaper. The canal traffic declined. By the 20th century half the canals had gone.

Ferrymen used to have boats to carry people and goods across rivers. They too were out of a job when railway bridges were built across rivers to carry fast trains in a few seconds. Today, **enthusiasts** are once again trying to clear weeds from the long-since abandoned waterways, to try to get barges running again —this time for fun.

Opening up the Midwest

The Midwest is the name given to about a million square kilometres of American territory between the densely populated eastern seaboard and the Rockies. Until the middle of the 19th century, it was the home of Red Indians and of gigantic herds of buffalo. Then came the white man, and he brought with him the new smoking monster, the train. Without railroads it would have been far more difficult to exploit the Midwest, and almost impossible to set up fast communications right across the Rocky Mountains and deserts to the Pacific Ocean.

The sometimes vicious battles between rival construction gangs were not the only danger to the railway-builders. In many areas, the Indians were hostile, and armed guards had to protect the workers from the attacking Indian bands.

Even after the lines were built they were not free from hazards and attacks. Natural hazards included the sinking into soft ground of hastily laid track, avalanches,

Left: *A modern freight crossing a bridge at Green River, Wyoming. Motive power is provided by a four-unit diesel-electric. The railway is the Union Pacific, and to show how far it has changed, the sketch (below, left) shows how in the early days the same railroad was used by passengers to shoot buffalo for fun from the train.*
The UP's first engine was General Sherman of 1865 (below).

deep snow drifts, shortage of water in the deserts, torrential flooding of great rivers (enough to carry away wooden trestle bridges), and falling stones, rocks and treetrunks after violent storms. On top of this came attacks by robbers who on several occasions held up complete trains and took the goods and possessions of passengers, just as highwaymen used to on the old roads in Europe. Twice trains were robbed of large sums of money, even though they had armed guards.

Even the respectable passengers did lasting harm. They took train rides lasting a week or more and shot buffalo for fun. Some train trips caused the death of as many as 10,000 of the great animals, and their dead bodies were just left to rot. After many years of this stupid killing it was discovered there were hardly any buffalo left. Today there are just a few herds, and they are strictly protected.

81

HOW THEY WORK

In the 19th century nearly all engines worked by steam, yet they differed widely in appearance. At first, the railways only wanted engines that would not break down, but later the call was for more power, to pull heavier trains faster. The railway companies also gave more thought to the amount of fuel the engines needed to do their job. Coal and wood, and later oil, got more and more expensive. Electricity provided the answer and the means to make expresses, such as the German Rheingold, below, extremely powerful.

Inside an Early Engine

Steam locomotives were among the first large products ever made by metal **engineering** methods. The only other big metal items manufactured nearly 200 years ago were bridges, and they did not have to be quite so accurately made.

When the first railway engines were built there were not many materials available from which to choose. Large and heavy parts were made of cast iron. In the case of **cylinders**, the massive casting then had to be 'machined' (shaped with cutting tools) to get the right size and shape. Other parts were made of wrought iron which, instead of being melted and poured into a **mould**, was heated and then shaped by men with heavy hammers. A few parts were made of brass, wood, leather and copper.

The early engineers had enormous difficulty in their early efforts to manufacture the engines. For a start, the boiler had to be able to turn water into steam at high pressure.

New ways had to be found to use the heat better; instead of just lighting a fire under the boiler, the flames and heat were carried in tubes right through the boiler to the chimney. The hot, high-pressure steam had to be controlled by valves, taken through pipes and made to push the **pistons** up and down inside the cylinders. Linking rods were needed to make the sliding pistons turn the wheels, and another linking system was needed to keep switching the steam first to one end of each cylinder and then to the other. Even getting the locomotive to work at all was not easy. There were no modern machine tools to make the parts accurately; a lot of the shaping was done by men with hammers and files. To stop steam escaping round the piston and piston-rod the gaps were packed with 'stuffing' made of rope and grease.

Right: *Perhaps the most famous locomotive ever built, Rocket (1829) incorporated such new features as direct-acting connecting rods, multi-tube boiler and blast pipes to make the exhaust steam draw the air through the fire.*

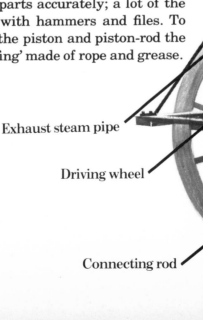

Chimney

Dome

Exhaust steam pipe

Driving wheel

Connecting rod

Right: *This simplified drawing shows how the piston oscillates up and down the cylinder and turns the driving wheel by means of a pivoted coupling rod. Steam is admitted first to one side of the piston and then to the other. The crosshead, fixed to the piston rod, slides up and down the well-oiled guide bars.*

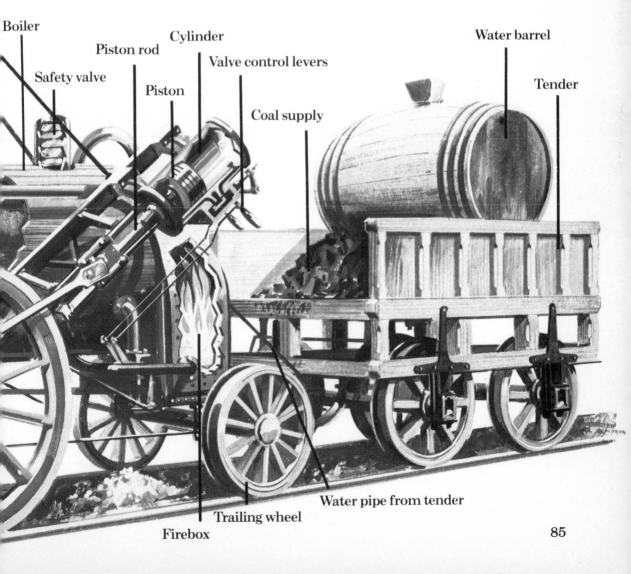

Boiler

Safety valve

Piston rod

Piston

Cylinder

Valve control levers

Coal supply

Water barrel

Tender

Water pipe from tender

Trailing wheel

Firebox

A Modern Steam Engine

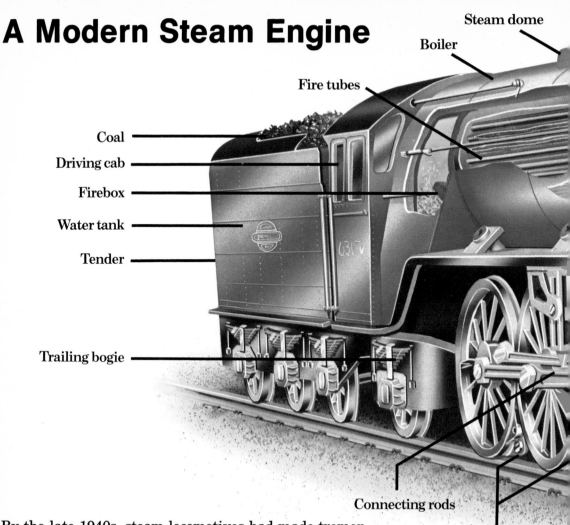

Steam dome

Boiler

Fire tubes

Coal

Driving cab

Firebox

Water tank

Tender

Trailing bogie

Connecting rods

Brake blocks

By the late 1940s, steam locomotives had made tremen-dous progress in technical performance since the Rocket. Yet although it looks quite different, the powerful 4-6-2 passenger engine worked in exactly the same way as the early steam engines. The differences were that it was much bigger and more powerful, and was made by modern methods (allowing far better accuracy) in stronger materials, mainly steel. This allowed higher boiler pressure to be used, to produce steam in large amounts to give higher power output.

Water from the tender was pumped into the boiler by the engine, but the stoker had to shovel coal to feed the fire. Flames curled round the brick arch and through the firetubes inside the boiler, to escape up the chimney. The steam above the water was led through a long series of 'superheater' tubes, to make the steam hotter and able to do more work. Then the superheated steam was allowed to **expand** inside the cylinders, working the pistons, before escaping up the blast-pipes which helped draw the fire gases through the boiler. The steam entered both

Above: *Final type of 4-4-6-2 for British Rail's Eastern Region, the Ivatt A-1 class was a good compromise between tractive effort and speed. Driving wheels of two metres diameter were turned by three cylinders each*

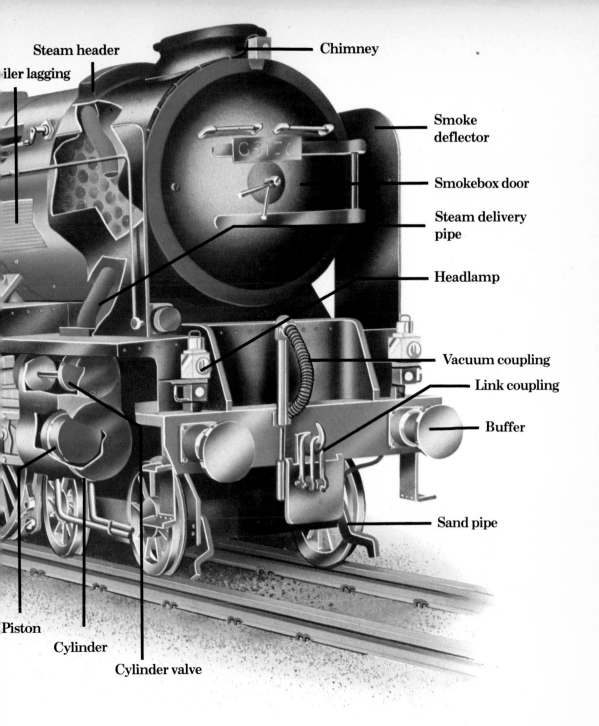

Steam header

iler lagging

Chimney

Smoke deflector

Smokebox door

Steam delivery pipe

Headlamp

Vacuum coupling

Link coupling

Buffer

Sand pipe

Piston

Cylinder

Cylinder valve

50 centimetres bore (piston diameter) and 70 centimetre stroke (distance moved by piston from front to rear). The A-1 had a tractive effort (pull) of 17,000 kilograms compared with 16,000 kilograms for the A-4.

sides of the piston and was controlled by the valve gear which, together with the **connecting** and **coupling rods**, formed 'the motion'. This could be seen in action as the locomotive moved along.

Some steam engines had three cylinders, one of them an 'inside cylinder' between the frames. Others had four, with two inside cylinders driving cranks on one of the driving **axles**. They were designed this way to make it easy to remove the parts for repair and maintenance work.

Inside a Diesel

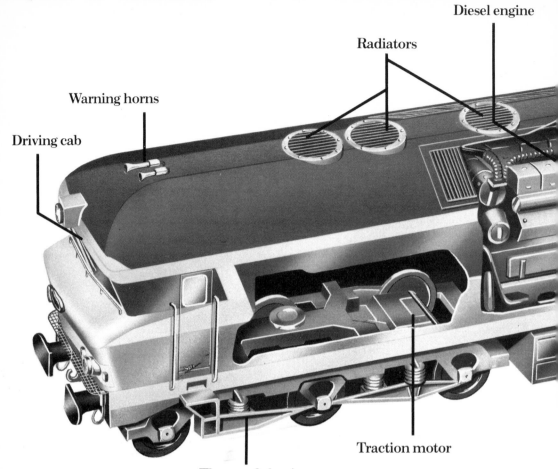

Diesel engine

Radiators

Warning horns

Driving cab

Traction motor

Three-axle bogie

Rudolf Diesel gave his name to the kind of engine used today in millions of railway locomotives, trucks, buses, ships and even cement-mixers. The diesel engine works like a car engine but needs no sparking plug for **ignition**. Instead, it causes air to be **compressed** inside its cylinders to such a pressure that it becomes extremely hot. Thus, when a tiny squirt of fuel oil is pumped in, it ignites at once by itself. Unlike a car engine, it does not need petrol but runs on various kinds of oil.

The diesel engine is very efficient, and does a lot of work for each litre of fuel it burns. It costs more to make than a steam engine, but because it is so much more efficient it actually costs less to run. That is why it has replaced most steam locomotives.

In a few small diesel locomotives the crankshaft of the engine is connected to the driving wheels, sometimes with a **gearbox**, as in a car. But in big and powerful

Above: *This diesel-electric locomotive shows how the main parts of such locomotives are arranged. Some have two diesel engines, but this has one large one, in the centre. Fuel is in tanks under the frame, and the exhaust is piped to the roof stacks through a turbocharger (a gas turbine driven by the exhaust) which compresses the air used in the engine.*

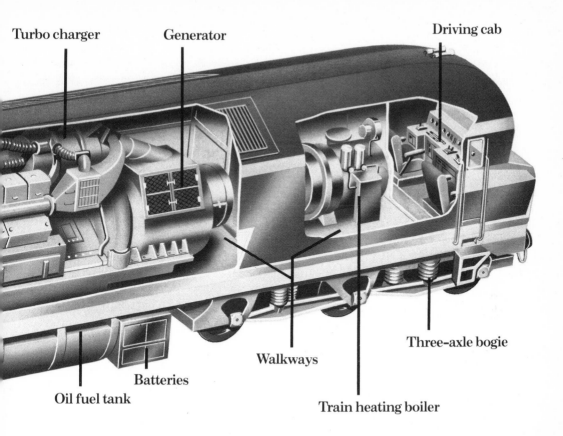

Turbo charger Generator Driving cab

Oil fuel tank Batteries Walkways Train heating boiler Three–axle bogie

Intercoolers cool the air before it reaches the cylinders. The engine drives an alternator (generator of a.c. electric current) which supplies traction motors geared to the driving axles. Electric cables are easier to connect to the swivelling bogies than high-pressure steam pipes. There is a driving cab at each end, so that the locomotive can run in either direction.

locomotives, this is more difficult to achieve. What is done instead is to use a diesel-electric drive system. The diesel engine drives an electric **generator**, and the driver controls the electric current supplied to 'traction motors' that drive the wheels. This is like having an electric locomotive that carries its power station along with it. A few diesel-hydraulic engines are also in use. These connect the engine to the wheels through a sort of gearbox that works by pumping oil in such a way that the speed of the train can be controlled without altering the speed of the engine.

Turbochargers are **turbines** driven by the hot exhaust gas. They put to use some of the energy that would otherwise be wasted, because the turbine compresses extra air fed to the engine. Properly adjusted, a diesel need not make any visible smoke, but most are very noisy.

On the Footplate

The footplate is the floor of a locomotive cab and, except in streamlined locomotives and most modern diesels and electrics, it ran right round the locomotive so that the crew could reach almost any part of it. On the earliest locomotives the footplate was nothing more than a plate for the feet. Sometimes it was dangerous; for example the driver of The Experiment could have easily caught his feet in the driving wheels.

There were hardly any controls or instruments in the early cabs, apart from a glass **gauge** showing the level of water in the boiler, and a lever to **reverse** the operation of the valve gear to make the engine go backwards. Of course, there was a door on the firebox to allow fresh fuel to be shovelled on the fire. Before long it became obvious that one man could not drive the train and keep his attention on the signals (you can read about signals on pages 148 and 149), as well as looking after the fire. It thus became normal to have a crew of two, a driver and stoker (called an engineer and fireman in North America).

By about 1855 almost all engines in North America had cabs to protect the crew from the weather and from soot, smut and cinders. Cabs slowly became common in Europe and gradually, too, the number of controls grew, but the steam-locomotive cab always remained harsh and uncomfortable. Usually the driver stood, grasping the **regulator** that controlled the rate at which steam was fed to the cylinders, and thus the power of the engine. There was no heating or cooling, but on a cold winter night both heat and light would come streaming from the open firebox doors. Still, there were few instruments, and the driver used his skill and experience to control the working of the engine.

Right: *The cab of the fastest steam locomotive of all time. Gresley's A-4 class of Pacifics were always extremely fast, but later ones went even better with their 'Kylchap' blast pipe and double chimney. One of the modified engines was Mallard, then numbered 4468, and in 1938 she reached 203 kph. Now, bearing her post-war number of 60022, she is in the Railway Museum at York. Her cab is just as it was when she was in service on the East Coast express route.*

Below: *Today few drivers are left who recall the days of steam. The controls in the cab of a 'steamer' are utterly unlike those of today's locomotives. In general a steam cab was harsher, less comfortable, and full of massive steel levers. Instruments were few.*

Vacuum gauge

Steam pressure gauge

Regulator handle

Vacuum brake controls

Reversing screw

Steam pressure gauge

Water level gauges

Regulator handle

Firehole and door

Hose for washing down footplate

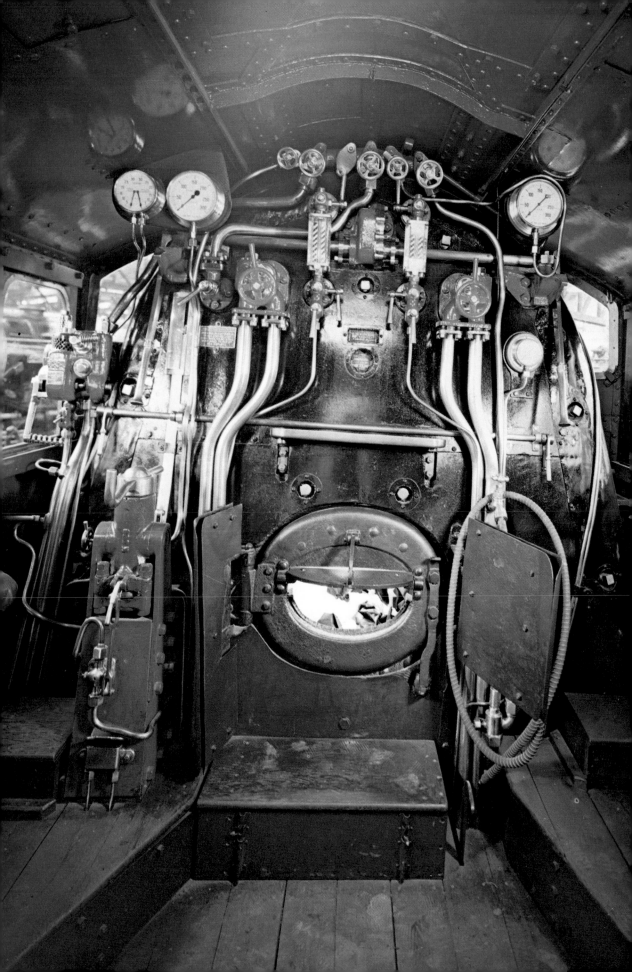

Advanced Passenger Trains

The Advanced Passenger Train (APT) is designed to run faster over ordinary track than any other trains in the world. Like many modern passenger trains, it is a 'multiple-unit' (m.u.) train, with no separate locomotive. Instead, there are engines or electric motors at **intervals** along the train. Some APTs are all-electric but, where the track is not electrified, the train is driven by gas turbines rather like smaller versions of the engines used in aircraft. The train is light and, by **accelerating** very

Above: *The APT cars are smoothly tilted to increase passenger comfort on bends.*
Left: *Inside the APT-E research train in 1973, showing the special test instrumentation that measures hundreds of vital temperatures, pressures, engine performance and even the behaviour of the bogies on which the cars ride.*
Right: *Cab of the APT-E marks a complete break with the traditional locomotive cab. Drivers of the future will need more technical knowledge but few muscles.*

fast, can keep up an extremely high average speed in excess of 160 kph.

From the start, the diesel and electric types of locomotive offered their crews a level of comfort that was never possible in the days of steam. The new engines were built more like passenger coaches, with windows all round and even with heating for winter and, in some countries, cooling in summer. The driver was given conveniently handy controls and plenty of instruments so that he could see just how the engine and train were behaving. (Steam locomotives often did not even have a speedometer.)

Comfort and neatness took a big step forward with the British Rail HST (High-Speed Train) of 1972, and the APT is even further advanced. In both these trains there is a single driver, comfortably seated behind a single large window of unbreakable glass. All controls and instruments lie at his fingertips and, if anything were to go wrong, he would be instantly informed by an **illuminated** warning display. Eventually, drivers will be in constant communication with other trains and with railway controllers (replacing today's signalmen) by means of electronic control systems. Even today, many drivers have a radio telephone communication system, though this does not work well in tunnels.

ODDITIES OF THE TRACK

Most modern trains look more or less alike. We easily forget how amazingly different steam locomotives used to be. Every possible idea must have been tried at some time or another, though very few of the really odd ideas actually worked. Some locomotives had huge driving wheels because it was thought this might be a way of making them go still faster. At least one had driving wheels so big that the boiler was put underneath the axle instead of in the usual place on top. The illustration below shows the curious Fontaine locomotive of 1880.

Travelling like a King

A century ago heads of state, who were usually kings, queens or emperors, travelled by train more often than today. Many had their own special railway carriage, and some had a whole train. Possibly the first royal coach was the one built for Queen Adelaide (widow of King William IV of Great Britain) by the London & Birmingham Railway in 1842. Though it had solid gold handrails and door handles, it had no heating and only two oil lamps for the three compartments. It could be made up as a sleeper for the night, but there was not enough room to lie full-length.

It was also in 1842 that Queen Victoria made her first rail journey. Eventually, she used many royal trains, and her main accommodation—two permanently coupled coaches—had no corridors. If she needed a lady-in-waiting the train had to be stopped, and the attendant called by a footman; the girl then walked along the track and had to be helped up the tricky steps into the royal coach. One of the coaches was the day saloon, and the other the royal bedroom. About 30 years after they were built, in 1895, the two cars were rebuilt into one big coach.

One of the most ornate royal saloons was that run by the Bavarian State Railways for 'Mad Ludwig' (King Ludwig II, though the train was actually built for his predecessor, Maximilian II, in 1860). The King's Saloon

Left: *Interior of Queen Victoria's royal saloon as it was in 1869. Later a corridor gave access for her dressers and other attendants, but there was never any communication with the rest of the train.*

was a rigid eight-wheeled coach, finished in richest royal blue and with gilding inside and out. Next to the royal coach was coupled the Balcony Carriage where the monarch received guests at the train's stopping places.

In contrast, British King Edward VII (1902-10) had his private coach finished comfortably but more simply, asking that it should be 'like a yacht'. His special carriage was assigned to the South Eastern Railway but kept on the Continent at Calais. His successor, George V, spent so much time in the Royal Train that he had a bath installed.

Above: *The adjacent saloon was the bedchamber of Queen Victoria and Princess Victoria. Today's traveller has greater comfort, though the space in a modern sleeper is much less.*

De Witt Clinton

Below: *The tiny Tom Thumb locomotive of the Baltimore & Ohio Railroad raced a horse-coach on 28 August 1830. The 'one horsepower' engine was winning when a belt slipped off a pulley.*

Named after a popular governor of New York, this engine looks quaint, but in fact it was a great improvement over Best Friend of Charleston (you can read about this engine on pages 20 and 21), which was made by the same firm (the West Point Foundry). Best Friend had an upright boiler, as did several other pioneer American engines such as the Tom Thumb of 1829. By 1830, it seemed that the **horizontal** boiler, as used on all the

Below: *The De Witt Clinton was one of the first American engines with a horizontal boiler (another was the British-built Stourbridge Lion).*

British locomotives from Trevithick onwards, was a better arrangement, and in the De Witt Clinton, the boiler was laid on its side. Unlike British engines, though, it was not covered with wooden slats, and the plates and rivets appeared very fragile (though they never burst). The fireman threw logs into the firebox from a large tender fitted with a lofty **canopy**, which strangely offered shelter only to the logs. Flue gases were piped through the boiler to a monster smokestack at the front.

At first glance no cylinders could be seen. What was not shown was that the four coupled wheels were driven by narrow sloping cylinders arranged inside the frame at the back. Here, the valve gear could be controlled directly by the driver. The **pistons** and connecting rods drove the front axle. On its first run on the Mohawk & Hudson Railroad, between Albany and Schenectady on 9 August 1831, this pioneer engine covered the 23 kilometres in 46 minutes, at 29 kph. It pulled a train of coaches looking like horse stagecoaches on rail wheels. Within another five years, American railway engines and coaches were beginning to look very different from anything that had gone before.

The Monster

The Monster was the name of a steam locomotive built in America in about 1834. The word monster is often thought to mean very large, but in fact it means anything that is deformed and unnatural. A monster could be quite small. This engine, however, was not only unnatural but it was also very big. It was, possibly, the first attempt in history to make a really powerful goods engine, able to pull very heavy trains. Since nobody had done it before, however, there was no way of knowing what was right or wrong. Later eight-coupled engines did not look so odd.

The designers of this monstrosity were Isaac Dripps and Robert Stevens, and the engine was built for the Camden & Amboy Railroad, in New Jersey. They chose an 0-8-0 wheel arrangement because they wanted a very powerful engine that would not slip with heavy trains

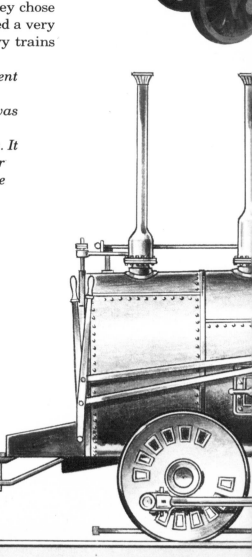

Right: *This drawing of The Monster is a copy of one made when the engine was new. The original artist may not have drawn the machine accurately because he has not shown any frames. Most steam locomotives had strong steel frames to which the wheels were attached by springs and on which the boiler rested. In The Monster everything seems to have been fixed direct to the vast boiler, including the wheels, cylinders, buffer beam, valve gear and footplate (through the floor of which was dropped a vertical pin to pull the train).*

Above: *One experiment in an eight-coupled wheel arrangement was the Buffalo, built in 1844 by Ross Winans. It had the upright boiler that was typical of the early American locomotive designs.*

and yet which had enough wheels to run over the rather poor track without breaking the rails. The difficulty with the 0-8-0, however, was that it was bad at going round corners.

The Monster had the biggest locomotive boiler then built, with a huge firebox, and a steam dome from which the steam was piped to powerful cylinders on each side. These were **inclined** and faced 'the wrong way', away from the driving wheels. They drove great swinging links, which in turn worked the complicated valve gear and moved the connecting rods driving the third pair of wheels.

Even more strange were the **couplings** between the eight driving wheels. The third and fourth pairs were linked by normal coupling rods. The third pair was linked to the second by gearwheels. Then another set of coupling rods linked the second and first pairs of wheels. But it worked.

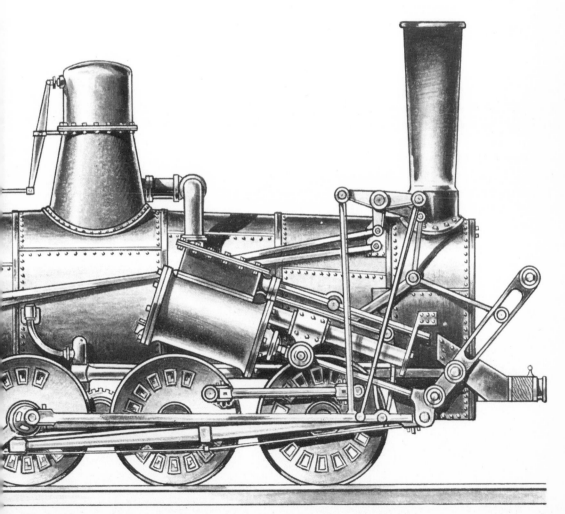

Atmospheric Railways

Though most people were excited by the new steam railways in the early 19th century, some wondered whether there might not be some better method to move people and goods on rails from one place to another. Diesel and electric **traction** had not been discovered, and steam power seemed the only alternative to the horse. But using a heavy, smoking locomotive that tended to break down or snap the rails seemed to some engineers a not very clever answer. They thought the steam engines should be in large houses beside the line, and bolted to concrete **foundations**. Some said they should pull trains by winding up cables on drums. A few thought of a less obvious method: they made the engine drive suction pumps that kept pumping air out of a large vacuum pipe laid along the track, between the rails. They then devised a way to make the suction pull a large piston along the pipe, and connect this with a train.

To make the piston move they sucked air out of the pipe in front of it and let **atmospheric** pressure in behind it (so such railways were called 'atmospheric' because they worked by atmospheric pressure). The first atmospheric line was built by two engineers named Clegg and Samuda on the Dublin & Kingstown railway in Ireland. The big pipe had a slot along the top, normally closed by a flap of leather. As a train went past the link between the piston and train lifted the flap and then shut it again.

The trains were silent and free from fumes, and passengers liked them. The London & Croydon was built next, in 1842-45, and, because nobody could find a way to make a junction with such a railway, the world's first 'flyover' was built. But when Brunel tried to use the atmospheric system in South Devon, from Exeter to Plymouth, rats kept eating the greased flap. After three years the rats won, and Brunel had to use ordinary locomotives.

Right: *Brunel, one of the greatest engineers in history, sometimes backed a loser. One of his mistakes was the atmospheric railway. As the 'engine' was pulled along by a remote source of power (the pumping station in the background) the train was quiet and free from fumes or soot.*
Below: *These diagrams show how the piston inside the vacuum pipe was connected to the 'engine' of the train. The two were linked by a coupling which ran along a slit in the top of the pipe. The slit was normally sealed by a flap (inset shows cross-section), which the train raised as it passed.*

Vacuum

Piston

Auto-Trains

What is a train? Does it have to have more than one carriage or wagon? With the auto-train railways were looking for a way to make light and cheap 'trains' to run over little-used branch lines. In the early days of railways branch lines went to almost every small town and village, and there was not enough traffic for proper trains. During most of the 19th century old engines and coaches were used, but a few railways made single-coach auto-trains. These consisted of an engine and coach joined together.

In the first one, built for the Eastern Counties Railway in 1849, the two parts—the engine and coach —looked quite normal, and the only odd thing was that they were all joined to the same **frame**. The tiny engine could just manage the coach behind it, and the unit shuttled between London and some villages to the north.

Later such 'trains' were called rail-motors, and came in various forms. In 1860, one had a tiny four-wheel engine with vertical boiler pivoted to the long coach. Then one was built for the London & North Western with the four-wheel locomotive inside the coach (which became very hot in summer). Eventually, such self-powered coaches were called railcars. A few had small

Below: *This auto-train of 1849 ran between London and northern villages such as Enfield (now part of London).*

steam engines tucked away, but most soon had diesel engines under the floor. Today the branch lines, in Britain at least, have all been closed because they cost too much to keep going.

Above: *Many auto-trains had the carriage body extended to enclose the steam engine. This one ran on the Taff Vale Railway in Wales.*

Stagecoach on Rails

It was natural that the first railway carriages, in America and in Britain, should have looked like stagecoaches mounted on railway wheels. But gradually designers thought again, and began to make them more like a box, and then like a long box with bogies at the ends, to carry more passengers. But until this happened there were some strange carriages.

The first Imlay-built carriages were single-deck 'stagecoaches'. Then, in the train first hauled by the De Witt Clinton, a few people sat on top, as in the old coaching days. There were no tunnels on that line, and the speeds were not high enough to bother the open-air passengers. But with the Imlay carriages built for the American Baltimore & Ohio Railroad in about 1832, passengers were being seated all over the coach. Inside there were three facing the front and three facing the rear. On seats at front and rear, on the ends of the coach, were another two groups of three. Finally, there were at least another dozen seated sideways on a long bench on the roof, under a tall canopy. It must have been a marvellous sight to see a whole train of such tall coaches swaying along, with the curtains streaming in the breeze.

By 1836, Imlay had noticed that even more people could travel in great comfort and convenience if seated in a long 'bogie coach' carried on four-wheel trucks like those being fitted at the front of American engines. His first such coach, called Victory, was built for the Philadelphia & Columbia Railroad.

Right: *This train of Imlay carriages makes a stirring sight, but there were obviously some drawbacks. High speeds were out of the question, and the billowing furnishings—and the crinolines of the lady passengers—must have caused difficulties in windy or wet weather. Today double-deck passenger cars are still much used in the United States, but they look completely different.*

The Hurricane

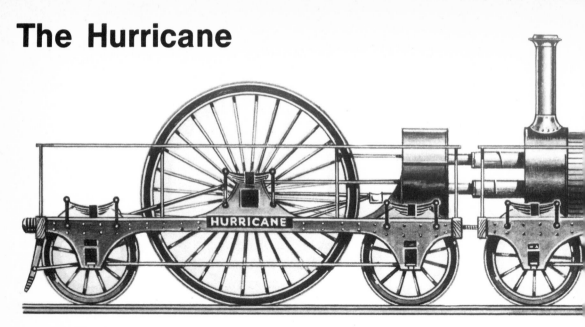

At first glance it is not too clear how the Hurricane locomotive works, and in some ways it looks less peculiar than the Monster. In fact, it was quite **radical** in design, and if the builders, R & W Hawthorn, had not made some basic engineering mistakes, they could have produced a first-rate engine far ahead of its time. As it was, Brunel soon regretted buying it for the Great Western Railway, along with its near-sister Thunderer, in 1838.

One of the basic difficulties with the traditional kind of steam locomotive is that all the parts fit so closely together that it is difficult to change one without affecting the other. For example, the boiler normally lies close above the driving wheels. To get more speed designers tried to make the driving wheels bigger, but (except for the Crampton which you can read about on pages 24 and 25) this pushed up into the boiler, so the boiler had to be smaller. By the late 1830s strange arrangements were being suggested to match big boilers to big driving wheels.

With Hurricane, the designer boldly took the driving wheels away from the engine and put them on a separate truck on the front, together with steam pipes and **exhaust** pipes connecting the cylinders to the boiler and smokebox. The engine itself ran on six small wheels. To build Hurricane, the Hawthorn company had to solve the tricky problem of piping high-pressure steam through **flexible** joints, because the driving vehicle had to be **pivoted** to go round corners. The weakness of the basic idea was that, with so little weight pressing it on the rail, the driving unit kept on slipping. Much later, a man named Garratt had the same idea of building a separate

Above: *The Hurricane is today regarded as just another of the stupid freaks that formed a 'dead end' in engine development. But in fact its designer was trying to do something quite sensible: fit a bigger boiler. Later this was done by Garratt.*

big boiler, but he wisely left off any wheels under it and made it press down on the driving wheels (you can read about this on pages 136 and 137).

Below: *Garratt engines supported their huge boilers on the driving wheels at each end, to get strong adhesion as well. This British one has a rotary coal drum.*

Steam-roller on Wheels

Looking vaguely like an old steam-roller, the Ajax was another of the strange steam locomotives accepted by Brunel in 1838 for his Great Western Railway. He was not a great steam-engine builder himself, and he may have been right to try out any novel design that looked promising, but it was bad business for the GWR. Brunel was a sound engineer, and it is surprising that several of his schemes turned out to be such complete failures (one was the atmospheric railway which you can read about on pages 102 and 103). With Ajax, and its sister Mars, he was still attempting to achieve really high speeds, and it seemed to Brunel that high speed was linked with enormous driving wheels.

These two engines were relatively large for their day, and quite powerful. By far the strangest feature was their huge driving wheels, each with a diameter of three

Above: *Sir Daniel Gooch was locomotive superintendent of the GWR and then chairman until 1889.*

Below: *Early locomotives of the GWR. Top row: North Star, 1837; Vulcan, 1837; Lion, 1838; and (in colour) Ajax. Bottom row: Fire-fly, 1840; Iron Duke, the first of a great class designed under Gooch and built at Swindon from 1847; and the four-coupled Lalla Rookh, 1855. It will be noted that none of these engines afforded any protection for the crew, though cabs were in general use in America by 1845.*

metres, the same as for those of the rival Hurricane. But, whereas the Hurricane had light **spoked** wheels, the builders of the Ajax and Mars decided to make the wheels out of vast sheets of heavy iron plate. This method was even used in the case of the four smaller wheels, though it would have been much simpler to make these with spokes. As a result, the Ajax and her sister rode very badly, and gave the track a terrible time because the wheels are the only part of an engine that is 'unsprung' and bears directly on the rails.

The giant solid wheels were also badly affected by strong sidewinds. Another rather odd feature was that bracing rods were needed in order to stiffen the heavy frame.

Soon, Sir Daniel Gooch of GWR was himself designing much better engines of less odd appearance. One of the most famous was Iron Duke, which in 1848 was running at an average speed of 107 kph, better than that of express trains in 1950.

Philadelphia

The Philadelphia was named for the American city where it was built, though the customer was the Vienna-Raab Railway of Austria, where it was delivered in 1838. It was a typical product of William Norris's works (you can read about Norris and his engines on pages 22 and 23), which set a fashion in having a long boiler, extremely tall smokestack, tall 'haystack type' firebox and single driving axle. Norris was particularly proud of Philadelphia. The wooden slats used as heat **insulation** around her boiler were not merely rubbed clean or varnished but painted in two-tone green. Then Norris sent out coloured pictures of the engine to impress possible customers. In 1838, a towering funnel was considered essential if the engine was to please likely buyers, just as later a passenger steamship had to have three or four funnels (even if several were dummies).

Coal needed a broader and shallower firebox with a large **deflector**, called a 'brick arch', to sweep the hot gases to the rear and then forward through the boiler tubes.

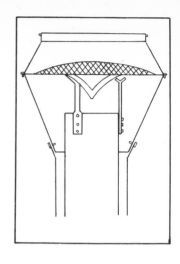

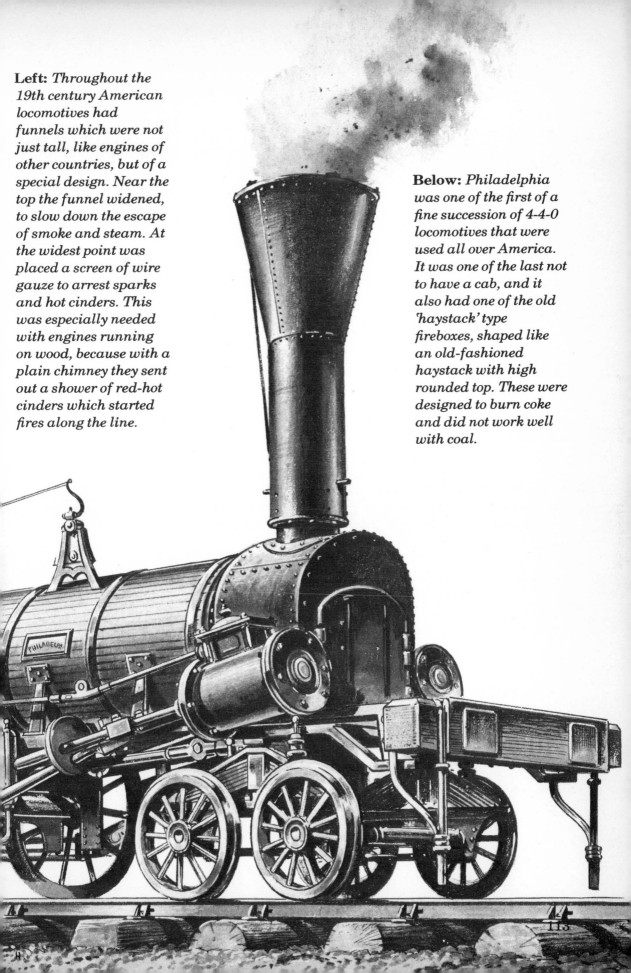

Left: *Throughout the 19th century American locomotives had funnels which were not just tall, like engines of other countries, but of a special design. Near the top the funnel widened, to slow down the escape of smoke and steam. At the widest point was placed a screen of wire gauze to arrest sparks and hot cinders. This was especially needed with engines running on wood, because with a plain chimney they sent out a shower of red-hot cinders which started fires along the line.*

Below: *Philadelphia was one of the first of a fine succession of 4-4-0 locomotives that were used all over America. It was one of the last not to have a cab, and it also had one of the old 'haystack' type fireboxes, shaped like an old-fashioned haystack with high rounded top. These were designed to burn coke and did not work well with coal.*

Meredith

The fantastically ornamental Meredith, perhaps the most colourful engine ever built, dated from 1850. This was a period when American railroads were painting their locomotives in vivid colours and covering them with a mass of elaborate design. Except for the black smokestack, almost every part of the engine was **embellished** with colourful paintwork, and some parts—such as the headlamp and its brackets, and the sides and windows of the cab now provided for the crew—were actually constructed in an **ornamental** way. This period of artistic design fairly soon faded from the American scene, to be replaced by a time when every part of a locomotive was painted solely in black. Even a white-painted number was welcome relief.

On the other hand, while British engines up to 1850 were often rather dull, the railways were soon painting their engines in bright and distinctive colours. This lasted until nationalization into one company made such distinctive colouring pointless.

Above: *Thomas Rogers was named after the head of the company which built it, in Paterson, New Jersey, about 1855. It was one of the fantastically embellished express passenger engines built in America in mid-century. Meredith was one of the engines which belonged to the Cincinnati & Chicago Air Line Railroad.*

Left: *An ornately-designed Meredith locomotive steams out of a country halt in the mid-1850s.*

The Meredith shows an intermediate stage between the 4-2-0 and the later and more powerful 4-4-0 models that pulled more than 95 per cent of American trains throughout the 19th century. The bigger and newer engines had a larger front bogie, with axles spaced wider to spread the load, but were otherwise much the same. Almost always the cylinders were on the outside. A 'cow-catcher' on the front, a large bell and a whistle were all considered essential; in Meredith, the whistle was perched loftily atop the huge brass steam dome above the firebox. The thing that looks like a dome was actually a sand box to feed sand under the driving wheels when necessary to prevent slipping. Another curious thing about US railroads at the time was to call themselves 'air lines' (Meredith belonged to the Cincinnati & Chicago Air Line Railroad).

Suspended Monorails

From the very earliest days of railways, inventors have busied themselves trying to improve on various forms of track. One of the alternatives to the usual track that has actually been put to use is the monorail (single-rail). One inventor showed how trains could run on a single rail, or even a strong cable, but nobody dared to build a full-size system, because it was thought people would be afraid to use it. Lartigue did build his crude monorail (you can read about this on pages 128 and 129). What is surprising is that the monorail proposals that did manage to get built were much more advanced than anything that had gone before. These were of the type that was suspended from an overhead rail. With this arrangement the rail is carried high above the ground on a series of posts or trestles, and the railcars or trains hang down under their wheels.

Above: *There was an odd blend of ancient and modern in the Meigs monorail proposed in 1886. The space-age cars would have been driven by steam along an elevated track.*
Left: *Modern suspended monorail in Japan.*

Above: *George Bennie Railplane.*

By far the greatest early monorail was that built at the end of the 19th century in a highly industrial part of West Germany, in what is today called Wuppertal. It ran 13 kilometres from Ober-Barmen, through the neighbouring town of Elberfeld to Vohwinkel. All the way, a succession of upside-down 'U' girders carried the two single-girder tracks well above the streets and rivers.

An even more extraordinary **suspended** monorail was built near Glasgow in 1929-33. The inventor was named George Bennie, and he called his cars railplanes. Each was hung from **tandem** pairs of wheels at the front and rear, running along a girder built into a rigid structure carried on steel towers. A second rail below the railplane connected with a sliding bracket to keep the car steady. At each end of the railplane was an electric motor driving an air propeller. During demonstrations speeds higher than 90 kph were reached, but though passengers liked this mode of travel, Bennie was unable to raise enough money to build a really useful length of track.

Right: *How many modes of transport can you see? This picture, taken in the German city of Wuppertal, shows the famous suspended monorail, as well as a main-line electric express, a three-car tram, a bus and a canal.*

Elevated Railroad of New York

To old New Yorkers, the 'Elevated', often just called the 'L', was the cheapest way of getting about the huge city, other than by walking. With London's hopelessly clogged streets as a warning, New York decided around 1855 to avoid **congestion** by building a system of local passenger railways carried directly above the streets on stilts or trestles. Later, it was also decided to copy London by building underground lines, but New York mostly lies on extremely hard rock which made this difficult and expensive. The Elevated was a much simpler and cheaper solution.

The Elevated was used by millions of commuters from 1870 until nearly 1960, when the last stretch of track was taken down. Almost the entire Elevated work was done by baby steam locomotives, all of them quite slow but able to pull very hard when **accelerating** from rest. This was vital, because the L's stations were only a few hundred metres apart. The earliest engines were of the 0-4-0 type. These had the special ability to go round the very sharp bends that had to be included to allow the line to go round the same corners as the streets below. Later the rather straighter Third Avenue line had bigger 0-4-4 engines and these became very popular. All the Elevated locomotives had comfortable **quarters** for the crew, called in America the engineer and fireman.

One class of locomotives for the NY Metropolitan line had cabs which enclosed the entire engine. The result looked like a passenger coach that had somehow got mixed up with a locomotive, especially since the styling of the coach was just the same as that of the passenger cars pulled behind it. These strange engines had extra **swivelling** single-axle trucks at each end to help spread the load and guide them round bends. In winter, the interior was kept pleasantly warm.

Left: *The steam-hauled Elevated was a familiar part of the scene in the bustling New York streets at the start of the 1900s. Today New York rapid-transit trains (inset) avoid the city streets.*

119

Push-me Pull-you

One of the most difficult problems facing designers of steam locomotives was how to make an engine that was powerful enough to pull heavy trains up steep **gradients** yet flexible enough to go round the bends in the line. If the track had been perfect there would have been no problem, because all the weight could have rested on one or two powerful driving axles. The difficulty arose because most railways, especially those with the steepest grades and sharpest bends, had rather poor track. The weight of the engine thus had to be spread over a great length, and this in turn meant an engine that could not go round sharp bends. There were two possible solutions: either railways had to use several engines on each train or designers had to find a way of making an engine that was both powerful and flexible.

Below: *One of the South American countries that bought Fairlie engines was Bolivia, which put this one into use in 1906. This class gave good service and, though the rail gauge was only 760 mm, it could pull heavy trains up steep mountain routes. The fireman had a busy time, because he had to keep two fires going at once, one on each side of the cab.*

In 1851, the Austrian State Railways held trials to find the best locomotive for the mountainous Semmering line. Two of the entrants had two sets of cylinders and driving wheels on one frame. One, the Seraing built by the Cockerill company in Belgium, had boilers facing front and rear, a cab in the centre and two sets of steam-driven bogies. An Englishman, Robert Fairlie, seized on this idea and eventually obtained a patent for it.

The Fairlie engine rode the rails rather like a bogie passenger carriage. The big bogie at each end comprised steam-driven wheels, usually of small **diameter**, while the **superstructure** usually looked like a pair of small tank locomotives going in opposite directions.

Many hundreds of 'double Fairlies' were built, mostly for mountainous lines in South and Central America. Their only real disadvantage was that they could not go fast, which on such routes would have been impossible anyway. The heyday of the Fairlies was 1880-1920, but some were built earlier.

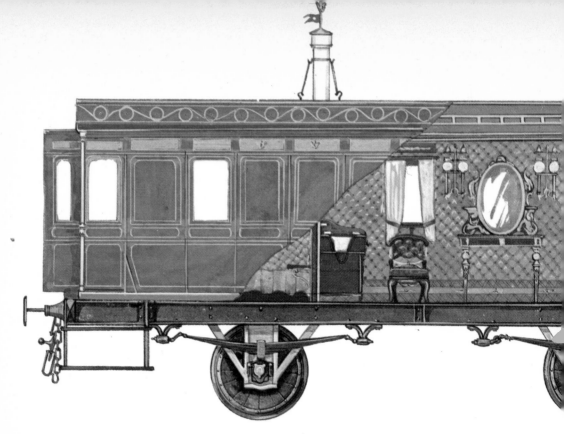

Era of Extravagance and Luxury

Outside Europe there were many people who had either their own lavish coaches or else their own train. Not all were heads of state. Some of the most luxurious passenger coaches ever built were for cattle barons, land dealers and other powerful men who, in the American 'Wild West', had suddenly gained immense wealth and decided they knew how to spend it. There were many tales indeed of the wine, women, song, card-playing, shooting and buffalo-shooting which happened on these private trains. Most of these fabulously equipped cars were built by the Pullman Car Company, which later hired out private coaches and trains to more respectable businessmen—sometimes for months at a time.

In 1856, the British firm of Sharp Stewart delivered to Said Pasha, Vice-regent of Egypt, a locomotive the foreign potentate had specially ordered. Said Pasha considered himself an expert on the way a locomotive should look, and the British painters carried out his instructions exactly, producing what was probably the most ornately painted engine in all history (rivalling the colourful Meredith which you can read about on pages 114 and 115). It was a regular 2-2-2 express engine, but embellished with intricate decoration, and the name

Above: *The Czar of Russia's coach was quite long but ran on only six wheels, without bogies. Like most of the 19th century royal coaches it was extremely ornate. It had a stove to keep it warm, but the interior did not look inviting by modern standards.*

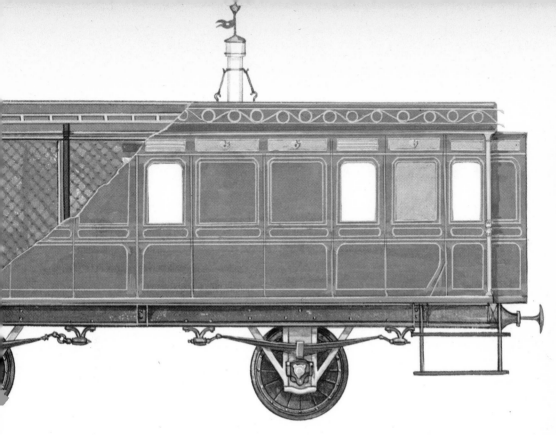

Saidia. (Sharp Stewart also made an extraordinary engine supplied to Portugal with 1-1-2-1-1 wheel arrangement.)

Three years later another firm, Robert Stephenson's, delivered an odd rail-motor to the Khedive of Egypt himself. This was not quite so ornate, but his majesty's personal saloon was built on the back, just behind the driver and fireman. Heavy drapes kept out the soot, sand and flies. Another British delivery of this time was the Imperial Coach for the Czar of Russia. It was surprisingly plain, and rather inconvenient, though it did have plenty of room and was well-insulated.

Below: *The government of Egypt probably had to pay almost as much for the painting of this locomotive as for the engine itself. It is reputed that the Vice-regent, Said Pasha, planned every detail of the decoration.*

Carving a Track through Snow

It was not long before railwaymen learned that deep snow can bring trains to a halt, and that there are better methods of clearing the line than shovels. All the earliest snow-ploughs (spelt 'plow' in North America) were simply very strong and heavy **deflectors**, shaped like a **wedge** or the prow of a ship, driven ahead by two or even three locomotives. Charging into really deep snowdrifts with three large steam locomotives all working at full speed was an exciting, and even frightening, experience. Once it was fatal. In northern England, in 1888, a massively built wedge plough sent to extricate the Flying Scotsman was rammed by mistake (during a blizzard) into the front of another train.

Above: *Typical of modern ploughs, this rotary type is seen at work on the national railway of the Soviet Union. At the rear are three diesel-electric locomotives.*
Left: *The earliest snow-ploughs were simple wedges, shaped to lift the snow and deflect it out to each side of the track. This one was used during the early years of the Northern Pacific in the United States (the photograph was taken in 1866).*

Where snow can be really deep a **rotary** plough has to be used, driven by power to fling the snow far to one side of the line. The first rotary ploughs, the Leslie design, were used by the Union Pacific and other American railroads before 1895. Most often they resembled a covered freight van carrying a multi-blade fan on the front, driven by a steam engine. Two or more locomotives would push the plough from behind, though without having to charge deep drifts.

In Switzerland, the Bernina Electric Railway used an extremely successful steam plough, because the power

124

Above: *Diagram to show three types of snow-plough. Right to left: Shallow plough attached to diesel engine; wedge-shaped plough for deep drifts and a modern rotary plough.*

needed could not be supplied by overhead electric wires. This plough had a single boiler, inside a van body, supplying steam to the driving cylinders and to the engine driving the fan-type cutter. Like modern diesel and electric ploughs, this one often cut its way through solid snow and ice, once to a depth of six metres, with glistening sheer walls. Modern ploughs are sometimes not of the rotary type but are instead an array of blades that carry the snow out to one side of the track. This is adequate for most snow, but for exceptional drifts deeper than the trains there is no alternative to the power-driven rotary type.

125

Marc Seguin's Engine

The Frenchman Marc Seguin is almost unknown today, and he was never famous throughout the world as were the British Stephensons. But in 1828 he patented a brilliant idea that improved the working of the steam locomotive and which also improved all other types of steam engine of the day. This was the multi-tube boiler.

Previous boilers were just iron drums full of water, heated over a fire. Steam was produced just as in a saucepan on a stove. Then, with early locomotives, the fire gases were piped through the boiler to a funnel at the other end. Seguin saw that steam could be generated faster if the gases were taken through the water in lots of pipes. This was done in almost every steam locomotive built afterwards, except for a few in which the boiler contained the fire and the pipes contained the water.

Left: *Marc Seguin imported engines from the Stephensons. He rebuilt them with multi-tube boilers, and then designed the engine* **below***. Hot gas from the fire travelled forward under the boiler and then back through the tubes to a funnel at the rear.*

But the engines built by Seguin were extremely odd. His first, built in 1829 for the St Etienne to Lyons Railway, had one of his excellent new boilers but it also pulled behind it a **tender** carrying huge fans. These acted like a bellows to blow fresh air through the fire. This worked quite well, but the fans were driven by belts attached to the wheels and this removed some of the power that should have gone into pulling the train. However, one feature of the train that the crew specially liked was that the footplate between the fans was warm and sheltered by a roof. Fans soon went out of fashion, however. Before long, designers learned to draw air through the fire by expelling the steam from the cylinders through a blast pipe pointing up into the funnel.

Listowel and Ballybunion

Listowel is a small Irish town on the railway linking Limerick and Tralee. Ballybunion is an even smaller place on the coast. Hardly anyone goes there, yet these little-known places were once linked by a railway that many consider to be the strangest ever built. If it were still running, visitors would flock to it, and Listowel and Ballybunion would very definitely be 'on the map'.

The two little Irish towns were chosen not because they needed to be linked by a railway but because the promoters of the strange railway simply wanted to find somewhere to build it in order to prove what it could do. The main inventor was a Belgian named Lartigue, and he had already built short experimental lines in his own country and in France. His idea was that in country areas it was possible to build track that was simpler and cheaper than ordinary railways, and would need no maintenance. He proposed a form of **monorail** (an ordinary railway is a bi-rail, or duorail) with the carrying rail held about 1·5 metres off the ground on a framework of steel girders. The locomotives and vehicles were all arranged to **straddle** this rail and hang down on each side, with steadying wheels on almost **vertical** axles running along guide channels on each side of the track.

Left: *Listowel and Ballybunion Locomotive No 1 about to move on to the turntable at Listowel yard, in Ireland.*

Above: *Front view of Locomotive No 1 in which the V-shaped rail can be clearly seen. The Listowel and Ballybunion railway worked well, but unfortunately it failed to make any money.*

The Listowel line was proudly opened in 1888. It worked perfectly well, and people came from far and wide to see it. Unfortunately, it never made money. One reason was that there was hardly any traffic available. Another reason was that the trains were most inconvenient. The odd locomotives were really nothing more than two little engines running side by side, but with a single driving axle carried high between them, turned by two baby cylinders. The main problem was that driver and fireman could hardly maintain contact with each other, and passengers on the right side of a carriage could not climb across to the left. Worse, loads were difficult to balance, and the story is told of the farmer who, wishing to send a cow to market, had to send two calves to balance it. The curious little line finally ended its days in 1924.

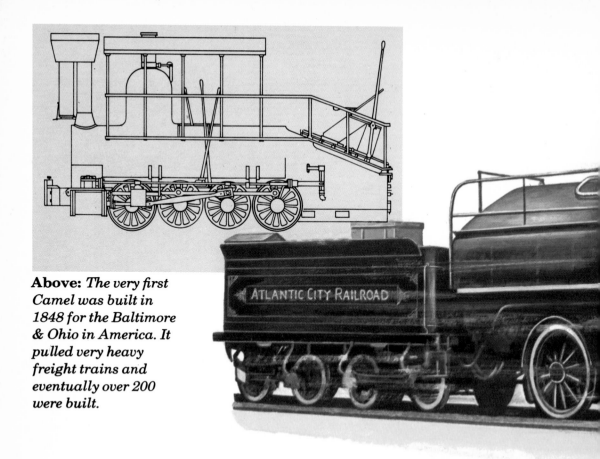

Above: *The very first Camel was built in 1848 for the Baltimore & Ohio in America. It pulled very heavy freight trains and eventually over 200 were built.*

Camel and Mother Hubbard

From the earliest days of steam railways it was normal to have a crew of two, both standing at the rear of the boiler. But it did not have to be like this. In 1900, the South Adriatic Railway (Italy) began to use 4-6-0 express engines with the cab at the front, the tender containing only water and the coal being in tanks on the sides of the engine. With oil firing it was even easier to put the cab in front, and the greatest Mallet compounds of the American Southern Pacific were arranged 'back to front' and were very popular. The main reason for putting the cab in front was to give the crew a much better view, without the obstruction of the boiler and smoke.

About 50 years earlier, Ross Winans followed his Mud-digger (which you can read about on pages 26 and 27) by the first of a very famous series in which the driver was moved forward right on top of the boiler. As he sat so high in the middle, like an Arab on a camel's hump, these odd locomotives were called Camels. Many

more were built by Samuel Hayes for the great Baltimore & Ohio Railroad. They looked strange, with everything heaped up in the middle; but they ran well until 1901.

By this time another arrangement had become popular throughout America. These were more normal-shaped engines, but they had the driver standing in his own cab half-way along, with the poor fireman out in the open behind his firebox at the rear. The driver entered his 'cupboard' through doors at front or rear, and usually had to stay on one side of the boiler. With express engines the driver did get a better view, but these Mother Hubbard engines were also built for slow freight and **commuter** traffic where the central 'cupboard' was covered in smoke and steam as often as if it had been at the back.

Left: *Early electric locomotives often had a camel-like appearance, with a high cab in the middle and sloping ends. This photograph, taken in 1896 on the Baltimore & Ohio, shows the first main-line electric locomotive in America.*

Mountain Railways

Railways specially intended for mountain work come in all shapes and forms. Some are electric, some have small diesel or petrol engines to work the trains, some are steam-hauled, and some are pulled by cables. In a sense, the cable-car is not a railway at all; the cables carry the weight of the cars, which may hang over an abyss 300 metres or more deep.

One of the obvious problems with mountain railways is steep **gradients**. Often smooth steel tyres will no longer grip, and the rack-and-pinion or funicular method is needed. The engine drives one or more toothed **pinions** (gearwheels) which engage the teeth in a rack between the rails. Another problem is that usually the gradient varies greatly, and at the bottom may be almost level.

If the incline is steep enough the engine and coaches have to be specially designed. Steam boilers may give trouble on a slope and are sometimes mounted upright. The Swiss Rigi Railway used steam engines with the boiler **inclined** up the slope and the cab at a different angle so that the crew floor stayed more or less level. The Swiss Brienz-Rothorn engines were all set at the same angle, to match the mountainside, and so looked very odd on level track. In the United States, the Mount Washington Cog Railway had a variety of strange engines, all of which looked very peculiar on level track.

Left: *A Zermatt-Gornergrat electric railcar in the Swiss Valais Alps.*

Above: *A much earlier mountain railcar was this steam one, looking like a staircase, built in 1889.*

The Swiss Pilatusbahn has always used self-powered carriages, at first steam and now electric, arranged like an enclosed staircase on wheels. Again, these look ridiculous on anything like level track, which as far as possible was avoided when the line was built. Opened in 1889, the Pilatus line is considered the steepest railway in the world with self-powered trains. The ruling gradient is one in two. This is far steeper than any road, and in fact would be extremely difficult to walk down if a road of this inclination were built. Britain's steepest line is the Snowdon Mountain Railway, which runs to the very summit. The little rack-and-pinion engines are the original ones delivered to work the line when it was opened in 1897.

Left: *Taken in 1874, this photograph shows one of the original steam railcars of the Swiss Rigi railway. Built in 1870, this was almost the first mountain railway in the world (an American line just beat it).*

133

Funnels without Sparks

Most transport vehicles have a central feature that becomes the main point of attraction. With a car it may be the radiator, while with a ship or a steam locomotive it might be the funnel. Steam locomotives without any visible funnel tend therefore to seem peculiar. Sometimes such engines were so-called 'fireless locomotives', built for use in explosives factories and other dangerous places where a single spark might cause disaster. Even modern diesel or electric traction might prove too dangerous in such areas. The fireless locomotive is a steam engine either filled with boiling water and steam already at high pressure, or else topped up from time to time with white-hot firebricks so as to keep producing steam.

Other steam locomotives had raging furnaces in the usual way, but still no obvious funnel. Jules Petiet, chief engineer of the Nord (northern) railway of France from 1845 to 1872, built many odd-looking engines in which the steam and flue gases were not allowed just to escape through the chimney, but were piped back through the top of the boiler to help heat and dry the fresh steam. The hot flue pipe also acted as a water heater, warming up the cold water entering the boiler and thus helping the fire to generate more steam.

There were many schemes for saving some of the heat lost from the funnel, but few produced such odd-looking locomotives as Petiet's. Many of his creations were tank engines in which the water supply was carried

Right: *Though it does have a funnel, this 4-4-0 compound of the Eastern Railway of France has a boiler with a steam cylinder on top.*

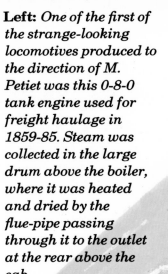

Left: *One of the first of the strange-looking locomotives produced to the direction of M. Petiet was this 0-8-0 tank engine used for freight haulage in 1859-85. Steam was collected in the large drum above the boiler, where it was heated and dried by the flue-pipe passing through it to the outlet at the rear above the cab.*

beside the boiler instead of in a separate tender. One, built in 1863 for hauling goods trains, had a 0-6-6-0 wheel arrangement, with separate front and rear sets of cylinders. This made the engine very powerful, but it needed a remarkable **array** of copper steam pipes and fat exhaust pipes running to and from the four corners of the engine.

Mallet and Garratt

While the Fairlie did well on narrow mountain routes, other designers found alternative ways of making steam engines powerful and flexible. Their locomotives were built in enormous sizes to carry out the biggest rail duties where the power was often needed simply to pull a gigantic freight train. The first was the French-Swiss engineer, Anatole Mallet, whose method was to mount an ordinary engine on two sets of driving wheels, the rear group being fixed to the frames and the front group being a pivoted bogie. As in the Fairlie (which you can read about on pages 120 and 121), this called for high-pressure steam pipes that were flexible. This required highly skilled engineering and it was not until 1890 that Mallet engines were fully successful. Then, without warning, they became enormously successful in the U.S.A. and by the First World War virtually all the most powerful freight locomotives being built for American railroads were Mallets. Most were 'duplex' (two sets of coupled wheels), and among these were the Big Boy class, the greatest steam locomotives in history (you can read about the Big Boys on pages 32 and 33). Others were 'triplex' (three sets of wheels, the front two groups being pivoted).

An important feature of nearly all Mallets was that their steam was **expanded** first in small, high-pressure cylinders and then in big, low-pressure ones. This improved efficiency, because each charge of steam was, in effect, used twice. The famed cab-in-front, oil-burning 2-8-8-2 Mallets of the Southern Pacific had 65-centimetre cylinders and 100-centimetre cylinders, the biggest ever used.

Above: *This great black freight engine of the former London & North Eastern Railway was the only one of its type to run in Britain. A 2-8-0+0-8-2 Garratt, it was designed by Gresley to work heavy mineral trains. Water was carried in the 'tender' at each end, but coal was carried only at the rear and fed to the large grate by a mechanical stoker.*

Englishman Herbert Garratt lived in Australia, where his first engine was built, a tiny 0-4-0+0-4-0. Nobody would have guessed that later Garratts would be giants, thundering across great continents with enormous trains which until then had needed two to four engines to pull. His scheme was to hang a boiler between two sets of driving wheels, usually by pivots at each end.

Below: *Cab-in-front 4-8-8-2 Mallet-type locomotive of the Southern Pacific Lines. It was built for hauling trains across the Sierra Nevada mountains.*

THE INDUSTRIAL WORKHORSE

From the dawn of civilization all man's land transport had been powered by his own straining muscles, and those of animals. The steam locomotive at last freed him from this work, though the fireman still had to toil to feed the hungry furnace. Today, the crews of diesel and electric locomotives sit in comfort, while their charges haul trains weighing thousands of tonnes. Modern trains are the most efficient form of overland transport that has ever been invented. Below are Union Pacific freight-trains at a crossover in Wyoming, USA.

Horsepower on Rails

The railway, it should be remembered, existed before the steam locomotive, and all the traffic at the early mining and quarrying railways, wagon-ways and tramroads, was drawn by horses. Even the renowned Stockton & Darlington began with only one steam engine, which operated in between large numbers of horse-drawn trains. Most of the horse trains were made up of either a short set of goods wagons or a single passenger coach. For several years the passenger coaches belonged to private individuals, who paid a **toll** to the railway for using the track. Most of the coaches were then hired out to the public, just as were the stagecoaches that ran on the roads. Only in the 1830s did the modern concept of a 'railway' become accepted, with the trains belonging to the railway and hauled by steam.

Until 1830, most of the railways belonged to coalmines, nearly all of them in northern England. Their purpose was to carry freshly mined coal from the pit-head to a barge or ship. Almost always this meant a downhill run from the mine to the quay. On many routes it was possible for the long train of coal wagons—either plain tubs or tipping **chaldrons**—to run the whole way simply under gravity. To stop the 'train', a man, the brakeman, had to ride on one of the vehicles and pull hard on the brake. At the back was a special wagon, called the dandy, in which rode the horse whose job it was to pull the empty train back uphill to the mine. Sometimes the horse also had to come round and be harnessed at the front for less-steep sections of the downhill journey. The horses soon learned where they had to pull and where they could ride.

Even as late as the 20th century there were still short lengths of track where goods or passenger vehicles were pulled by a horse. In some countries rail wagons are still shunted or pulled by buffaloes, mules, horses and camels.

Above: *The coalmining areas of north-east England were the setting for some of the first industrial railways. This picture was drawn in 1773; the horse did not have a 'dandy' and had to walk behind the loaded chaldron.*
Left: *Flanged wheels, very like those of today, were fitted to the first chaldrons hauled on the Stockton & Darlington in 1825.*
Right: *Flanged-wheel chaldrons were used as early as 1815.*

From Road to Rail

The first railway passenger trains often carried road coaches. In those days wealthy people owned horse-drawn carriages or coaches, just as today we own cars. If their owners wished to go on a long journey they often galloped the coach to the station, had the horses taken out, and waited while the coach was loaded on to a rail flat-car. Then the occupants would get back into the coach and ride to their destination, where fresh horses would be waiting.

This convenient practice took years to die out, despite one or two catastrophes caused by the fact that particular carriages had not been securely tied down. In France, the road-rail concept was taken further by building coach bodies for transport by either rail flat-car or a road **chassis**. The best-known example was a large coach intended for public use as a road-rail bus, with a coachman seated on top and three interior compartments for up to 24 passengers. On the road it ran on a regular chassis, with front wheels on a truck pivoted to the shafts for the four horses. A special **transfer** yard was provided

Above: *This Freightliner depot on British Rail is equipped solely for handling container freight. Each container is transferred between trucks and trains by specially designed gantry cranes, with grabs that match the sockets on the corners of the containers.*

Below: *Today the soaring costs of transport are partly held in check by containerization. This means packing freight in standard boxes for carriage by ship, trains, road or air.*

where an overhead **gantry crane** hoisted up the coach body and gently lowered it into position on the railway flat-car.

Precisely the same method is used today for much of our rail freight. The ISO (International Standards Organization) container is a large box specially designed to clip securely on to either a road or rail flat-car, or into a ship or large aircraft. In the United States, the old French road-rail idea is followed even more closely with the trailer train. The biggest road freight trucks comprise a diesel engine with an **articulated** trailer to carry the load. The trailer is driven from the factory to a railroad freight depot, where the trailer is uncoupled and hoisted by a large gantry crane on to a rail car. The trailer train covers the main part of the journey much faster and cheaper than by road. At the destination yard, the trailer is unshipped and coupled to another diesel engine which pulls it to its final destination.

Below: *Probably the earliest example of specially designed 'inter-model' transport was this scheme for carrying a passenger carriage on either road* *wheels, behind a team of horses, or a rail chassis for coupling onto a train. This French scene of 1835 has counterparts in today's Motorail.*

Moving the Big Loads

From the beginning, railways have always been able to carry loads too heavy to be easily transported by road. Of course, the loading gauge sets an upper limit on a load's size, but specially bulky loads can sometimes be carried by using a train at a less busy time with the load arranged to hang over the adjacent track. Occasionally this means removing and then replacing a few signals, telegraph poles or other obstructions, as in the case of the biggest loads carried by road.

British freight trains were for many years unable to transport the heaviest loads. One reason was the small loading gauge, which restricted goods wagons and loads to sizes much smaller than in North America and some other countries. Another problem was that the wagons had no brakes, so the guard's van, or brake van, had to provide all the braking at the rear of the train, working in skilful partnership with the engine crew at the front. It was inefficient, because going down a long gradient the train had to be braked hard all the time; if it had been allowed to run freely it would have been impossible to stop in emergency. Despite these problems large wagons were in use long before the end of the 19th century, including 40-tonne well wagons for bulky loads (such as

Above: *This picture of the Union Pacific Railroad shows triple layers of new cars being delivered.*

Right: *This picture was taken at Doncaster, England, about 1900. It shows one of the most famous express types of the Great Northern Railway, a Stirling eight-footer (2.5 metres driving wheel) mounted on a specially built well-wagon. Well-wagons are low-slung to allow big loads to clear the loading gauge.*

Top right: *Heaviest normal freight cars on British Rail are tankers. These 100-tonners carry liquid nitrogen at minus 196°C.*

a large steam boiler or even a locomotive) and 40-tonne coal wagons with discharge hoppers in the floor. Both types of wagon weighed about 56 tonnes fully laden.

Today much bigger loads can be carried. In 1865, William Adams of Britain introduced an improved bogie which became standard on heavy freight cars all over the world until British Rail research workers devised a new one in the 1960s that runs smoothly at over 240 kph. Vehicles with these bogies today range up to 30 metres in length. Possible loads for a single rail vehicle today can be 150 tonnes of molten steel, a flock of 250 sheep on two decks, 32 small cars fresh from the factory, or an electric transformer weighing over 200 tonnes. The heaviest load ever carried was a steel tube (for a refinery) which weighed 436 tonnes, carried 1,120 kilometres in the USA in 1963.

Freight in Bulk

Today, the world's railways are fighting a constant battle against rising costs. It is a general rule of all transport that costs can be held down if more traffic can be carried, and this is true for both passengers and freight. Another basic factor is the 'cost of labour'; in the old days men received low wages, but today labour costs are very high. This has brought about a revolution in transport and particularly on the railways.

In the 19th century, goods trains were made up of many small trucks. Each truck carried only a small amount, but it all had to be loaded by hand. Often ten men might spend all morning loading one small goods wagon. Then an army of men called shunters might spend a whole day assembling trucks into a complete goods train. The train would proceed on its way at about 24 kph, stopping frequently in sidings to let expresses go past or to have wagons taken off or added. At any time there could be thousands of goods wagons standing idle in sidings and yards, some of them not moving for months on end. Whenever a wagon reached its destination, another large gang of men would have to unload it. Today, with high labour costs, such methods would be far too expensive.

Nowadays, railways carry freight in gigantic wagons and do all loading and unloading mechanically. Bulk commodities such as coal, oil, grain, iron ore and ballast are poured or pumped in at high speed. To unload, either **shutters** are opened in the bottom of the body or else the contents are blown out by air pressure from a hose connection. Many **commodities**, such as meat or fresh fruit, need to be refrigerated (or sometimes kept

Left: *This train of Canadian National Railways has freight cars marked to show the items carried.*
Above: *Modern electric power stations consume*

146

vast amounts of coal. Some need 44 trains such as this, with 1,000 tonnes of coal, moved every day on British Rail.

warm), and other rail trucks have special shockproof **chassis** and **couplings** to avoid damaging particularly delicate loads. Bulk coal or gravel, on the other hand, is just tipped out by rolling the whole car right over. New motor cars are carried thousands of kilometres on three-deck transporters, made up into trains carrying anything up to 1,000 cars.

Marshalling Freight Trains

The old method of using dozens of men to sort out small goods wagons, shunting them up and down small yards with the help of baby engines—or even horses, or manpower—has today given way to the modern marshalling yard. Such a yard is an enormous open space, often three kilometres or more long, covered with many rail tracks arranged side-by-side and all joined by points at the ends of the yard. The purpose of a marshalling yard is to keep as many freight vehicles as possible earning their keep in running trains laden with goods. No longer can railways afford to have thousands of wagons standing idle. As soon as a freight train comes to its destination it either turns round and goes back—as in the case of express container trains—or it goes into a marshalling yard to be reassigned.

The whole train is driven over an artificial hill called the hump. As it approaches, each truck, van or other vehicle is automatically inspected. One inspection device is a remote-control TV camera, which shows the vehicle to the controller sitting in a distant room very much like the control tower at an airport. Another instrument reads all the letters and numbers and other information carried on a small panel on each car. A third device may weigh the car, and in some places, wherever vehicles have been running at speed, electronic instruments report if any of a train's hundreds of axle bearings are running hot (which would indicate failure).

At the top of the hump each car is automatically uncoupled, and it starts to roll downhill. The controller presses switches which divert each car along its correct track. As it rolls, its speed is slowed down by automatic braking devices built into the track. Finally, the car gently nudges the end of a fresh train and is automatically coupled on. Often there are 'up' and 'down' yards on each side of the main railway route, and with powerful lights the work of marshalling goes on 24 hours non-stop. Freight cars may be marshalled empty or full, but the result is always the same. Out of the yard flows a succession of fresh freight trains, each made up of exactly the right number of vehicles in the right order.

Right: *The humpmaster's tower in the foreground dominates the computerized yard of the Santa Fé line at Barstow, California.* **Inset:** *Inside the tower.*

Right: *'Hump' shunting dispenses with the need for shunting or 'switching' locomotives by letting wagons roll down an incline. Each train is gently pushed over an artificial hill, and the uncoupled trucks roll down, one by one.*

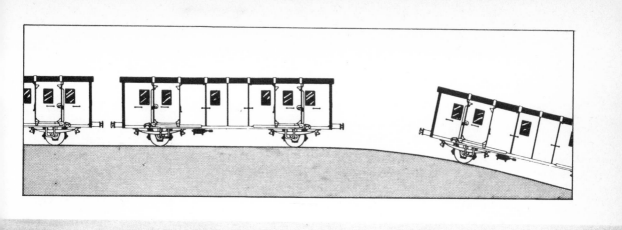

149

Specialized Cargo

Railways have to be able to carry almost anything. Old locomotives going to a museum may rub shoulders with a millionaire's yacht, valuable animals on their way to a zoo, 10,000 refrigerators, army tanks, day-old chicks or the morning newspapers. Any load that has to be carried regularly is packed neatly and loaded **mechanically**—for example, by fork-lift truck or a conveyor belt—and the most welcome load of all is the standard container. The 'container revolution' which got under way in the 1950s enables goods to be packed securely inside steel containers and carried by road, rail, sea or air and never unpacked until the container reaches its destination. But many loads cannot simply be put inside a container; they often demand special care in transport.

Above: *Part of a long flat car on the DB (German Railways) showing containers for Aral fuel.*

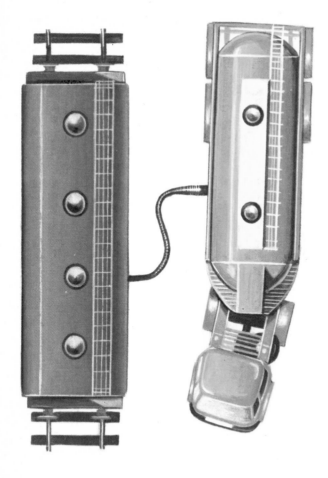

Above: *In recent years the transport of powdered materials, such as cement, has been speeded by blowing it by compressed air through a pipe.*

Below: Another special DB freight carries Marder armoured vehicles for the German Army.

Apples can be carried in large quantities, because tens of thousands can fit into a large rail van and as many as a million in a train. But they have to be safely stowed in strong boxes able to support the weight of a high column of boxes resting on top. In summer, the van has to be refrigerated, but in winter it may have to be kept warm.

Zoo animals and young chicks also need special treatment; like people, they need to be kept at a comfortable temperature. On the other hand, molten steel poses a very special temperature problem. Special 'torpedo' wagons can carry as much as 100 tonnes at a time. At the destination the 'torpedo' is carefully turned over to pour out its contents into receiving ladles. The metal of the container is protected by an inner lining of firebrick or other **heat-resistant** material such as magnesite. A protective coating is also needed by chemical tankers, which are often lined on the inside by a layer of glass.

Liquids are usually simple to pump in and out, but in recent years engineers have developed ways of pumping other materials such as sand, powdered cement, wet cement, fertilizers and animal foodstuffs. Today, material such as powdered cement can be blown at the rate of almost a tonne a minute to a height of 23 metres, to the top of a concrete mixing plant.

151

Train Ferries

While the earliest railway builders often had to bridge rivers or canals, and build viaducts across deep valleys, they sometimes came to water barriers too wide for the railway to cross. Coal wagons were ferried across large rivers on barges as early as 1842, and in 1850 a specially designed train ferry began operating in Scotland across the wide Firth of Forth, followed by another across the Firth of Tay a year later. Both were eventually replaced by great bridges. In Canada, a ferry began operating across the St Lawrence between Quebec and Levis in 1915, but this again was only needed until 1918 when the Quebec Bridge was opened. But there are many ferries across open seas, where no bridge or tunnel is ever likely to be built.

There was never any great difficulty about making a ship carry a train, but in some places there are problems in running the train on board and off again. This is because of the tides. The first large train ferry, the Leonard, which used to cross the St Lawrence at Quebec, had to contend with differences in water level as great as six metres. The three rail tracks were therefore mounted on a great steel deck carried on vertical guideways and raised or lowered by ten pairs of **screw-jacks**, driven by a special steam engine. As a result Leonard looked fantastic, with a vast criss-cross shaped superstructure, funnels like those of a power station, and a train seemingly supported in mid-air. This remarkable ship also had to serve as an ice-breaker in winter, as do the train ferries in the Baltic and other marine areas which freeze over in winter. But the Baltic, Mediterranean and several other important seas have little or no tides, so it is easier to drive trains on and off.

The longest international ferry routes take all day or all night, and sometimes passengers make the whole trip whilst asleep in a sleeping car. Obviously, it is necessary to avoid too many bangs and bumps whilst loading or off-loading, and during the sea journey the train has to be kept comfortably heated. Some of the most important ferries, from Britain to Europe, originated during the First World War, when the need arose for specially equipped hospital trains to be sent to France.

Right: *Sleeper cars of the Night Ferry go aboard at the British port of Dover. Next morning the passengers wake up in either Paris or Brussels.*

Right: *A diesel shunter pulls freight cars off the ferry Christian IV at Kristiansand, in Norway, after crossing the Skaggerak from Denmark.*
Below right: *Loading a high-speed ferry at Dunquerque with freight cars for Britain. In the winter 1976-77 the cross-Channel ferry services were improved by better port facilities and new freight vehicles.*

152

TRAINS AT WAR

From the mid-19th century railways have played a major role in warfare. Along the metals of a dozen railway systems have rolled trains of troops, tanks, strategic supplies, hospital trains, gigantic guns too big to be moved in any other way, and armoured trains which looked like long, mobile fortresses like the one seen below which is being attacked by a German gun emplacement. In 1943-45, the Allied air forces mounted such a campaign against Hitler's railway system that hardly a train could move anywhere in Europe.

The General

The American Civil War, fought between the Federal forces of the Union in the north and the so-called 'Rebel' forces of the Confederate states in the south, was the first conflict in which railways played a major role from beginning to end. By 1861, when argument finally changed into fighting, until the defeat of southern forces in 1865, the Union's bigger and better railroads were an important factor in their ability to move quickly their troops from one place to another. From the Great Lakes to more than 1,600 kilometres south, on the Gulf of Mexico, the Federal railroad system moved men, guns and supplies in such a way that Confederate forces were always outnumbered.

For the first time, railways not only did military duty but became military targets. By mid-1862, the Confederates had blown up the Cumberland River bridge, raided and destroyed the important railroad depot at Manassas Junction, Maryland, and derailed dozens of Federal trains. Some centres changed hands several times, and each time the defeated troops destroyed everything possible before they withdrew. Even such large cities as Chattanooga, Vicksburg and Atlanta were captured and then recaptured, with trains often playing a central role.

Above: *This mortar—a short-range howitzer that lobbed heavy cannon-balls—was called 'Dictator' and became famous for its exploits on the Petersburg railroad.*
Below: *Reinforcements for General Johnson take a tumble as a train is derailed in the forests of Mississippi.*

Right: *The famed General.*

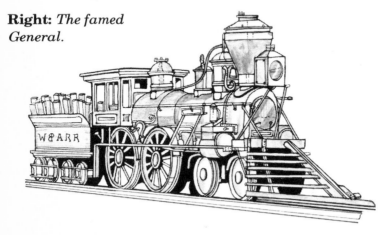

The most exciting locomotive chase in history took place in April 1862. A party of Federal troops led by Captain Andrews fought their way deep into the Confederate state of Georgia to try to cut communications between Atlanta and Chattanooga. They dashed into the station at Kennesaw, 48 kilometres north of Atlanta, and grabbed the General, a 4-4-0 express engine. Opening the throttle, they roared away to the north, destroying every-

Below: *At the end of the war in 1865 the roundhouse (engine sheds) at Atlanta looked like this.*

thing in their path. But some Confederate troops chased after them in the Texas (running backwards, because there was no time to turn round), and after a wild race over 140 kilometres of track they caught the General just 32 kilometres from Chattanooga. Both these famous engines are now in museums.

Railway Strategy

Though the first military railway in history was laid by the British during the Crimean War in 1855, this ran only a few kilometres and was soon removed. It was Bismarck, Chancellor of Prussia, who first realized how important railways could be in warfare. Around 1860, he planned the swift construction of a network of major rail routes throughout Prussia and the many neighbouring small German states. This great rail system was specially designed for use in war. Bismarck saw that, with the totally new **mobility** railways could give his armies, he could defeat any surrounding country and also unify the whole of Germany. In 1866, the Prussians put their railway system to its first big test. There was soon a war with Austria and this led to the defeat of the Austrians. Four years later came an even bigger test. Prussia declared war on France, heavily defeated the French armies and besieged Paris before France surrendered.

On an even bigger scale, British engineers were at

Above: *During the Second World War the German railways built enormous numbers of standardized freight locomotives called Kriegslokomotiven (War Locomotives) which today are still found working in many countries. At the top is one of these 2-10-0 engines near Etzelwang, West Germany. The other picture shows a Kriegslokomotiv at Izmir in Turkey.*

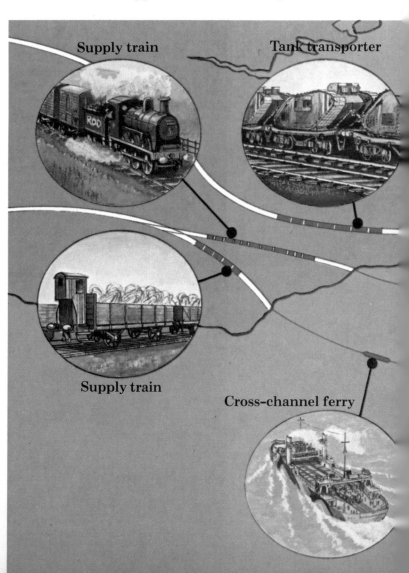

Supply train

Tank transporter

Supply train

Cross-channel ferry

Below: *During the First World War railways were the chief source of supply for the Western Front. In addition to existing lines, thousands of kilometres of new railways were built to carry millions of men and vast tonnages of munitions. Narrow-gauge light railways took supplies right into the front line.*

the same time building a rail system on a gauge of 1.06 metres intended to run 9,600 kilometres from Cape Town to Cairo and on into Palestine. This was as important for commerce and trade as it was for war.

The 'Cape to Cairo railway' was a grand Imperial design which was never realized, though the 1.06 metres network does today cover most of Africa. Parts of the system were involved in military actions soon after they were completed. In upper Egypt, in 1882, a rebellion was put down by the first armoured train. In 1898, the campaign in the Sudan was supplied entirely by the British military railway from the Red Sea, which was now within reach because of the Suez Canal. A year later the Boer War brought home to everyone the vital importance of railways in military conflict. It showed beyond doubt the value of trains in giving an army mobility over great distances, with sufficient supplies. It also showed how easily a railway can be attacked by even a small team of brave saboteurs.

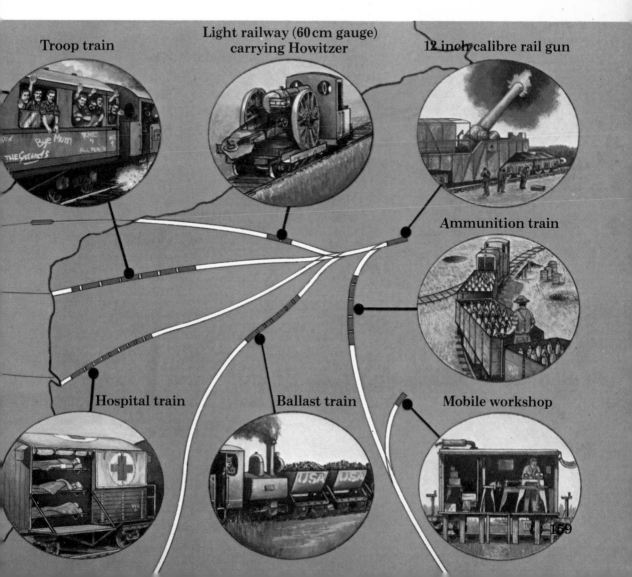

Troop train

Light railway (60 cm gauge) carrying Howitzer

12 inch calibre rail gun

Ammunition train

Hospital train

Ballast train

Mobile workshop

The Line That Died

It was not only the British who used railways to control their empire. The Germans and Turks in the First World War were united as the Central Powers and they, too, strongly supported the growth of railways throughout their empires. At the dawn of the 20th century, they were busy constructing a new railway to run from Turkey southwards for hundreds of kilometres through the Middle East and on into Arabia, to Medina. Here was to be the terminus, partly to serve the military and partly to carry thousands of faithful pilgrims each year to visit the Islamic holy city of Mecca. The gauge was 1.04 metres, and the engineers and all the equipment were German.

Construction got under way in 1901. The Hedjaz Railway, as it was called, reached Amman (today the capital of Jordan) in 1904. Two years later it got to Tebuk (today Tabuk) in the Hedjaz, and in a further two years, in August 1908, the line had reached its terminus.

Early in the First World War, a young British army officer, T. E. Lawrence, obtained the permission of General Allenby to form and lead a great band of Arabs on raids against the Turks and, in particular, the Hedjaz Railway. In many exciting battles 'Lawrence of Arabia' and his faithful followers brought heavily armed trains to a halt, killed or captured the occupants and reduced the trains to scattered wreckage. In a dozen places the track was completely destroyed. Gradually, Lawrence's force worked north, while the regular British army pushed back the Turkish armies, capturing Jerusalem and eventually approaching Turkey itself.

The entire 850-kilometre southern section from Amman had been so thoroughly destroyed by Lawrence's wild Arabs that the wreckage strewed the desert for 45 years. Eventually, the Jordan State Railways managed to re-open the line as far south as Ma'an, but it was not until 1963 that a British company was given the contract to try to clear the old rubble and get the southern section operating once more.

Above: *Sketch of Lawrence of Arabia by the British artist Augustus John.*

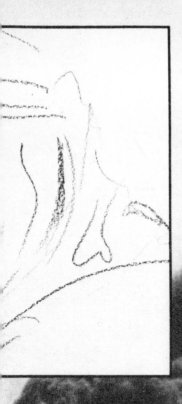

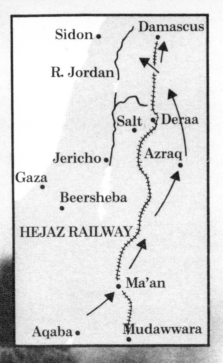

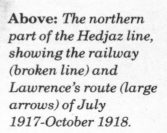

Sidon •

R. Jordan

Salt •   • Deraa

Jericho •   • Azraq

Gaza •

Beersheba •

HEJAZ RAILWAY

Ma'an

Aqaba •   Mudawwara

Damascus

Above: *The northern part of the Hedjaz line, showing the railway (broken line) and Lawrence's route (large arrows) of July 1917-October 1918.*

Left: *An explosion blows one of the German-built locomotives off the line as the Hedjaz Railway feels the weight of Lawrence's attacks.*

Armoured Trains

An armoured train is a very practical tool of warfare, because trains are easily able to carry a great weight of armour that would be an impossible burden for most road vehicles. The first armoured train was a hastily constructed vehicle created to help restore law and order in Egypt during the nationalist rebellion of 1882. During the battle at Tell-el-Kebir at the start of the troubles, two British navy officers mounted a '40-pound' gun and some Gatlings, manned by Royal Marine infantry, in goods wagons, armoured with steel sheet. Rows of sandbags protected the boiler of the locomotive. This train played an important part in the advance from Alexandria towards Ismalia and Cairo.

During the Boer War (1899-1902) the British (and the Boers) used much more advanced armoured trains which operated over hundreds of kilometres of track from Cape Town up through the Orange Free State to the Transvaal. Though stifling in summer, these well-protected trains were almost impossible to attack by the Boer marksmen. The trains both protected the track against saboteurs and carried supplies and wounded. Some were fitted with army artillery or naval guns, while others included cars for injured troops or for prisoners of war.

Left: *A famous photograph showing the first armoured train. Hastily contrived in 1882 with a gun and armour from HMS Hecla, it helped bring peace to Egypt.*

162

Above: *Boer riflemen are seen opening fire on a British armoured train built in Cape Town. It was used to keep the line open from Belmont to the Modder River..*

Above: *Certainly the first big gun put on a railway truck, this 152 mm naval gun took part in the Boer War of 1899-1902.*

When the First World War broke out there were fears of an invasion by German forces of the English east coast. One of the plans considered to deal with this possibility was a decision to build an armoured train. This would speedily bring artillery and troops to the scene of a foreign landing. The London & North Eastern Railway works at Doncaster converted the 0-6-2 tank engine, while the London & North Western works at Crewe built the train. This turned out to be a major assembly of heavily armoured bogie cars carrying naval guns in swivelling turrets, riflemen and stores.

In the Second World War there were many armoured trains, most of them used by German and Italian forces over large areas of Europe. Some were escorts for special troop or prisoner trains, some bristled with anti-aircraft guns from end to end, and some of them carried large, long-range guns.

The Rail Gun

In 1918, huge shells travelling faster than sound exploded in the heart of Paris, though there were no Germans within 109 kilometres. In 1941, similar shells caused tremendous damage and many deaths in Dover and Folkestone, in England; they had come across the Channel, from France. Such attacks could be made only by gigantic guns, and such guns could move in only one way: on railways. The rail gun was a very special item of warfare, whether looked at as a weapon or as a piece of railway rolling stock.

Some of the first big rail guns were originally built for use in battleships or fixed land fortresses. It was one of these, with a calibre of 38 centimetres, that the Germans used to bombard Paris. They gave it a new barrel so that it could send shells as far as 122 kilometres. But the greatest railway guns of all were

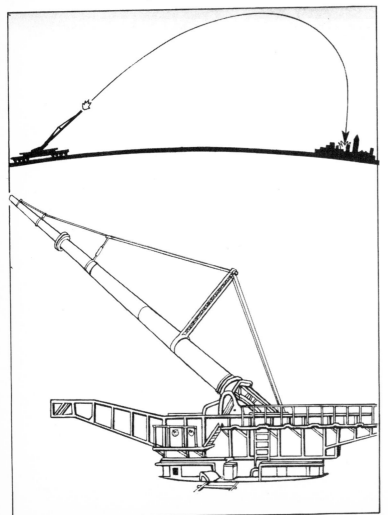

Left: *The Paris Gun had a barrel so long it had to be reinforced with bracing wires and struts, to stop sagging which would have made its shells fall short. The upper illustration shows the trajectory, the path taken by the shells. Each projectile climbed through the atmosphere into the stratosphere, the thin air above a height of 12 km, where resistance to the shells was much reduced. Then they plunged steeply onto the target.*

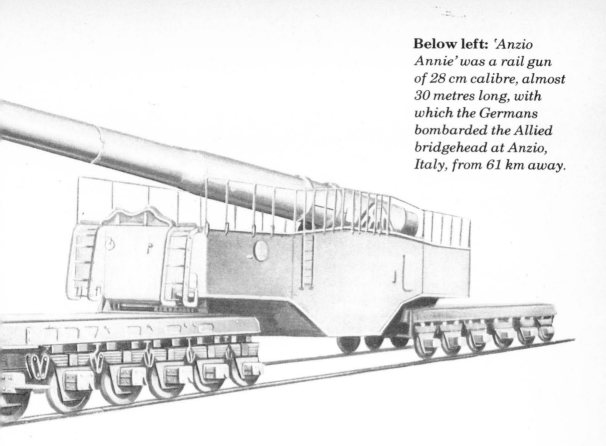

Below left: *'Anzio Annie' was a rail gun of 28 cm calibre, almost 30 metres long, with which the Germans bombarded the Allied bridgehead at Anzio, Italy, from 61 km away.*

built in Germany before and during the Second World War. The guns that shelled England were of 21 centimetre **calibre**, and were called Kanone 12 (cannon No. 12), but there was one monster gun that dwarfed everything else ever run on a railway. In 1937, the giant Krupps arms firm decided to build for Hitler the biggest gun in the world. It was called Gustav, after the head of the firm, and it had the gigantic calibre of 80 centimetres. Each of its shells was 7.62 metres long, and their weight varied from four and three-quarter tonnes for the ordinary high-explosive type to seven tonnes for special ones to pierce concrete and armour. The whole gun weighed 1,329 tonnes, and needed a crew of from 250 to 1,420 men commanded by a major-general.

This stupendous gun was so big it had to be taken to pieces in order to fit the railway loading gauge. It incorporated large cranes to put itself together, and then load itself with shells. But Gustav was so huge it was not ready to break through the French Maginot Line in 1940. Once, in the Soviet Union, one of its shells blew up an ammunition dump protected by being 30 metres underground. But the most amazing thing about Gustav is that this vast mass of solid steel simply vanished during the war. No trace of it has ever been found!

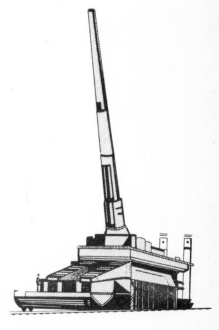

Above: *The world's biggest-ever gun, Gustav, seen during tests in Germany.*

Second World War

Unlike the static trench warfare of 1914-18, the Second World War was a war of movement. In just nine months, the German armies had swept across Europe and were in control of western France, eastern Poland, the Low Countries and even Norway. By 1941, the Germans had engulfed European Russia and the Balkans. This meant that a gigantic railway system which had formerly belonged to 17 countries was now being used to carry **munitions** for the German war effort.

During the first two years of the war, the mighty railway system continued to run efficiently and expand quietly. It was a different situation for the railways of Britain, which were blasted constantly by bombers of the Luftwaffe (German air force). But in 1943 the Royal Air Force began to retaliate. Soon, vast fleets of bombers were raining down on European industrial centres thousands of tonnes of high explosive every night. They made a special point of aiming for rail centres and **marshalling yards**. By day, British and American fighters swept far afield, attacking every passing train with cannon fire, bombs and rockets. By 1944, trains were bristling with flak (anti-aircraft guns), but the attacks increased and became more ferocious.

Once a Mustang fighter was destroyed by the explosion of the train it was attacking: the whole train had been filled with warheads for flying bombs. By 1945, no length of track could be used for a greater distance than a couple of kilometres.

Above: *By 1945 nearly every rail marshalling yard in Europe looked like this. Air attack had brought the German-controlled rail network virtually to a halt.*

Below: *Any train that dared to run in northern Europe in daylight was almost certain to be bombed or attacked with rockets by Allied aircraft. No aircraft did more such work than the Typhoon.*

GREAT RAILWAY SYSTEMS

The brief act of driving in a golden spike when a railway line was completed told nothing of the years of toil by thousands of men to build the railway. Whole armies of navvies laboured through mountainsides, in jungles and deserts and even across frozen plains to provide the means for people to travel in comfort to their destinations. The toil of those men meant that a network of shining steel would stretch around the world. Seen below is the French turbotrain, one of the great trains of the world.

Changing Pattern of Railways

Partly because of competition from air and road travel, the pattern of railways has changed. Apart from local lines in cities (you can read about these on pages 180 and 181), most railways get the bulk of their **revenue** from freight. Some, including those newly built in Mauretania (Africa) and Labrador (Canada), exist only to carry one **commodity** such as iron ore. Areas containing dozens of coal mines require a dense net of railways, because nothing else could handle the tonnage. For example, in Yorkshire (England), coal traffic is immense; the biggest electric power stations there consume 9,500,000 tonnes of coal a year, which means 44 trains of 1,000 tonnes serving one power station every day. With modern freight traffic everything possible is done to cut down costly man-power. Wagons are identified, sorted and, in the case of minerals such as coal, loaded and unloaded entirely by automatic equipment.

The heaviest freights in North America often need as many as ten locomotives, some of which are half-way along the train or pushing at the rear. All are electrically controlled from the cab of the leading unit. In the old days of steam, extra 'banking engines' were often added at the back to push heavy trains up steep inclines, but for fast passenger trains it was generally thought too dangerous to push from behind. This was because it was believed the coaches would jump off the track. On test runs, however, it was shown to be quite safe. Today push-pull working is common. On the Chicago, Burlington & Quincy Railroad, for example, suburban **commuter**

Above: *Senegal is one of many African nations where the railway was planned and run by Europeans. Today it is a completely national operation. This train is at Bamako.*

Above: *The highest railways in the world are found in the Andes mountains in South America.*

Above: *In remote regions the railway is often the settler's only link with the outside world. This 'Tea and Sugar' train brings supplies to people in desert areas of Australia.*

Left: *Passenger trains all over the world are increasingly being worked by 'multiple unit' stock: there is no locomotive, and the coaches are self-powered. Some m.u. trains have diesel engines under the floor, but this very modern example in London runs on electric power.*

trains with enormous double-deck cars of gleaming stainless steel are pulled by a diesel out from Chicago to stations on the line to Aurora, 60 kilometres west, and then (without turning round) pushed back to Chicago at over 128 kph. Expresses on Britain's Southern Region from London to Southampton and Bournemouth have three sets each of four cars. The four cars at one end have electric traction motors of 3,200 horsepower, and they pull the other eight out of London and push them back.

It is in the less-populated and often bleak terrains that the train has become a vital part of man's need to overcome natural barriers in order to stay in contact with his fellow men. Trains today are an important means of communication in such diverse **environments** as the Arctic snows and steamy tropical jungles. In many parts of the world they are the only way to maintain surface **communications**, and though aircraft are often used by more passengers the train can carry bigger loads more cheaply. People who live in countries criss-crossed by good roads should remember that very few countries have any paved roads at all, except in cities, and the railways are the only alternative to the aeroplane, the canoe or the ox-cart.

Trans-European Express

Faced with such severe competition by cars and buses for short journeys, and aeroplanes for longer journeys, the passenger train has had to make tremendous improvements to keep attracting customers. When the Second World War came to an end the European railways were left in a terrible state, with smashed track and old, worn-out trains. But during the next few years the nations of Europe, conquerors and conquered alike, took the opportunity not only to rebuild the railways but to link the networks of different countries so that travellers can go as easily and quickly as possible all over the Continent. The aim now is to carry passengers in ease and comfort between cities as fast as they could go by jet (because, unlike the jet, the train goes right to the centres of the cities, where most passengers would prefer to arrive). The trains that do this are called TEE, for Trans-Europ Exprès (or, in English, Trans-European Express).

Each TEE train has smooth, quiet-running bogies and extremely comfortable air-conditioned coaches. Over 100 cities are on the TEE network (covering all of western Europe) and a computerized reservation system means that every ticket is sold for a vacant seat—nobody ever has to stand. Though all sorts of people use the TEE expresses, they were specially intended for businessmen, and most are timed so that busy people can make a trip to a distant city between about 8 a.m. and noon, have a 'working lunch' and do an afternoon's business, and then travel home between about 6 and 10 p.m. Many TEE trains provide telephones, secretaries able to speak several languages, and various other business necessities (such as office facilities) and even barber shops.

At first, most of the TEE trains were diesel railcars, or multiple units (trains with engines built into the coaches), or hauled by diesel locomotives. They could not be electric because different countries used different sorts of rail **electrification**. But during the 1960s engineers began to build extremely powerful electric locomotives that can pick up the different kinds of current from each system and convert it to the sort needed by their **traction** motors. Some are 'quadricycle' engines, able to pull the train at 160 kph on 1,500-volt direct current (Holland and parts of France), or 3,000-volt direct current (Belgium, Italy and parts of Luxembourg), or 15,000-volt alternating current (Austria, Germany and Switzerland) or 25,000-volt alternating current (new track in France and Luxembourg).

Right: *The TEE route network has grown to link all the major cities of central and western Europe. The busiest TEE routes are Paris-Brussels and along the Rhine from the Ruhr (the Duisburg/Dortmund area) south to Frankfurt and Mannheim. If the Channel Tunnel had been built London would have joined the network*

172

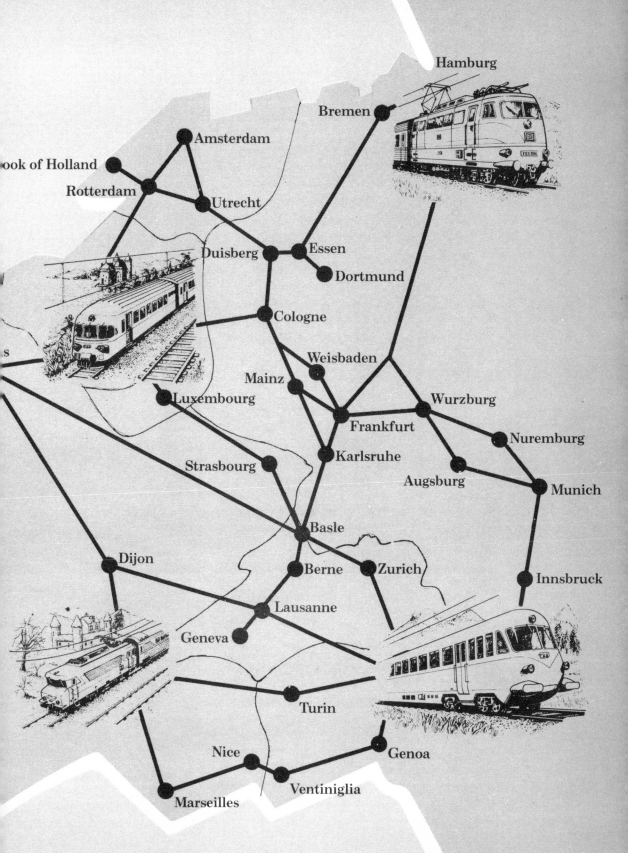

Hamburg

Bremen

Amsterdam

ook of Holland

Rotterdam

Utrecht

Duisberg

Essen

Dortmund

Cologne

Weisbaden

Mainz

Luxembourg

Wurzburg

Frankfurt

Nuremburg

Strasbourg

Karlsruhe

Augsburg

Munich

Basle

Dijon

Berne

Zurich

Innsbruck

Lausanne

Geneva

Turin

Nice

Genoa

Marseilles

Ventiniglia

173

Comfort and Convenience

Inside a modern coach a passenger's surroundings are much more comfortable than the interior of even a royal saloon 100 years ago, and they are better designed and require less attention. In fact, the change is as great as the change inside an ordinary living room. Today we like uncluttered rooms and we use different materials from those used in earlier decades; instead of mahogany, silk and brass we use aluminium (so-called satin-finish), shiny stainless steel and rotproof plastics. We also make use of a whole range of new woven fabrics built into upholstery made by new methods with foam rubber instead of horsehair.

Railway coaches are different too, with bodies made like a jetliner out of strong but light panelling of aluminium **alloys**, stainless steel, glass fibre and special 'sandwich' materials that were unknown in the old days. Today engineers know how to design coaches so that they do not jerk about, but instead ride smoothly even at the highest speeds. Railway designers have also found ways to cut down noise as well (continuous **welded** rails help because they cut out the traditional clickety-clack noise of running over rail-joints).

In the United States, a century ago, the last coach of a passenger train was usually an observation car, open at the rear. Since then many trains have specially-built coaches added on the back. This gives passengers a good all-round view, but today the passenger on many railways can get an even better view from a vistadome car. These were first used in the United States more than 40 years ago and are now found on most European railways and a few in other parts of the world. By building a long domed lounge to the full height of the loading gauge, and lowering the roof of the rest of the coach, passengers can have a panoramic view in all directions.

Right: *The two photographs at near right show the amazing contrast between the interiors of passenger coaches over the past hundred or so years. The upper photograph was one of the first ever taken in a train, and shows a three-tier sleeping car on the Great Western Railway of Canada in 1859. The lower scene was taken in a sleeping car of The Canadian, the crack transcontinental train of today's Canadian Pacific (CP Rail) also shown* **far right**.

The Swift Tokaido Bullets

Most railway enthusiasts have heard of the New Tokaido Line. It is in Japan, and the reason for its fame is because it is the fastest, as well as the busiest, ordinary rail route in the world. This is because, compared with most railways, it is completely new. Most of the world's high-speed trains have to run over routes that were planned 100 or more years ago. These routes have sharp bends, badly designed junctions where speed must be reduced, busy centres with complicated signalling, and even such problems as old underground colliery workings or ancient viaducts where speed must be held to a safe limit. In contrast, the New Tokaido Line was planned from the start for speeds of at least 240 kph. Despite the fantastic rise in Japanese air travel, the line was built to link the existing Tokaido Line (which was unable to cope with the traffic) with some of the biggest cities in the world—Tokyo, Osaka and Yokohama among them. At a cost of thousands of millions of dollars a completely new rail route was laid out, with no sudden rises or descents, no level crossings, few stations, no bend with a radius less than 3,000 metres and with a minimum of junctions or other disturbances.

The New Tokaido is 638 kilometres long. To run over the best track in the world the Japanese National Railways built a great number of 'Bullet' super expresses, constructed like jetliners and driven by electric motors totalling more than 12,000 horsepower in each train. The result is a series of passenger expresses whose speed is breathtaking. Every day 56 trains run non-stop from Tokyo to Nagoya, 367 kilometres, in exactly two hours; this means an average speed of 185 kph, and at times the 'Bullet' streaks along at 255 kph. In between run 56 semi-fast expresses, stopping at all six intermediate stations, a journey that takes two hours and 41 minutes, an average of 136 kph. The time for the complete 638-kilometre journey, including stops, averages 250 minutes, equivalent to 165 kph. Such performance costs money. Each night the 'Bullet' wheels are reground to the exact tyre profile, and the track is inspected carefully. Problems were found in sudden air-pressure changes on entering tunnels and old-fashioned toilets also had to be replaced by a sealed type. But the New Tokaido is the busiest line in the world, and it makes a profit.

Right: *The New Tokaido Line links several of the world's largest cities.*
Below: *The 'Bullet' trains are called Hikari (Lightning) in Japan. Each has 16 coaches and carries about 1,000 passengers on average. There are no signals on this line; a special control system protects the racing trains, just 15 minutes apart!*

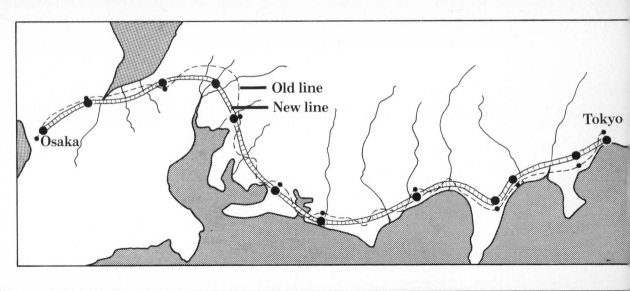

Old line
New line
Osaka
Tokyo

Underground Railways

The first underground railway was built in London nearly 120 years ago to allow people to get about more easily than they could in the traffic-choked streets. Even though the trains and stations reeked with **sulphurous** smoke—which many passengers thought was good for their health—the new underground line was very popular and made a profit from the start. So more underground lines were built, and in 1870 the first deep line was opened. The earliest routes had been built by the 'cut and cover' method: workmen dug a huge trench and then put a roof over it. The new deep line was much more difficult to build and passengers had to go further down to reach the trains (at first using lifts and later **escalators**), but it could be routed anywhere the planners wished, without disturbing the city above it. In 1896, Glasgow had an 'underground', Boston had a 'subway' in 1898, in 1900 Paris opened its first 'Metro', and since then about 25 other cities have followed suit.

The first electric underground line was opened in London in 1890. The coaches had hardly any windows, so a conductor (guard) had to walk up and down the train shouting the names of the stations. Today undergrounds are pleasant places and the trains are light and airy, though in the morning and evening 'rush hour' they become packed with commuters (people who travel to and from work in the city). In Tokyo, special attendants on the platforms push passengers into the overcrowded trains. Such trains would not work if they did not have stations close together, trains following at frequent intervals, and coaches with unobstructed interiors, lots of standing space and sliding doors controlled by the driver or guard. In fact safety is increased if the whole railway is made as automatic as possible, and in London a completely automated underground line was opened in 1927 to carry mail between big post office centres. Now several cities, led by London and New York, have automatic underground passenger railways, though none has yet had the nerve to do away with a human 'driver'.

In 1966, Paris introduced a costly 'super-Metro' route with trains running on complicated bogies having rubber-tyred wheels, as well as the ordinary metal wheel. For most of the journey the train runs on its rubber tyres, but at points and junctions the flat concrete strips on which the tyres run, are allowed to slope away downwards, bringing the ordinary wheels down on to the steel rails.

Above: *Newest of London's underground routes is the Fleet Line, here seen under construction. It will open in 1977.*

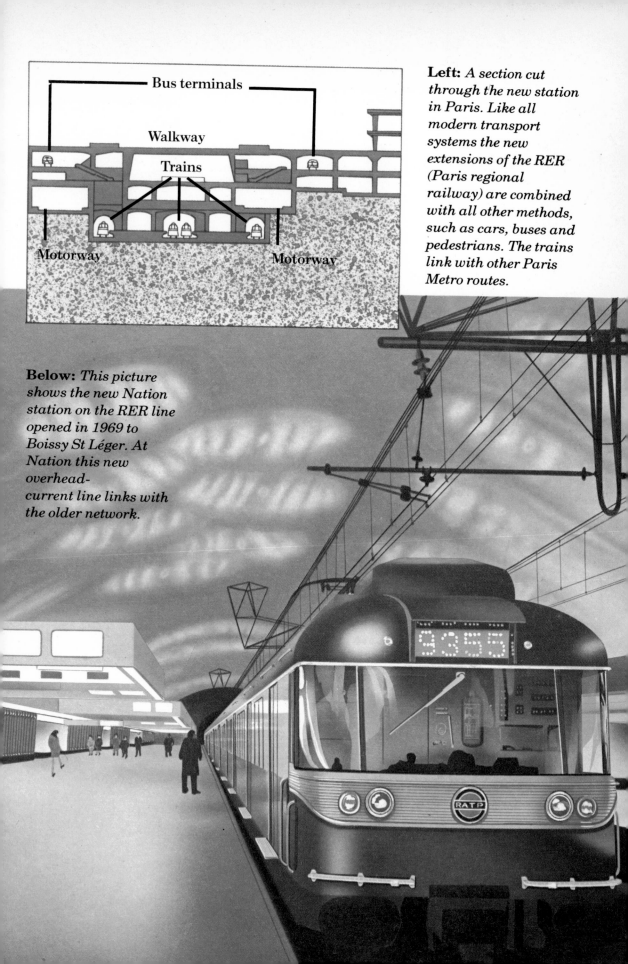

Bus terminals

Walkway

Trains

Motorway

Motorway

Left: *A section cut through the new station in Paris. Like all modern transport systems the new extensions of the RER (Paris regional railway) are combined with all other methods, such as cars, buses and pedestrians. The trains link with other Paris Metro routes.*

Below: *This picture shows the new Nation station on the RER line opened in 1969 to Boissy St Léger. At Nation this new overhead-current line links with the older network.*

Tickets, Platforms and Stations

The first railway tickets were sold from a room in a small house on the Stockton & Darlington line, but when the Liverpool & Manchester Railway was built **architects** were given the job of designing something quite new: a railway station. They also had to create railway maintenance and repair shops, turntables for turning engines round to face the other way, and eventually had to devise other railway systems such as signals. Stations started by looking very much like houses, but they had to incorporate a way of keeping people off the railway unless they bought a ticket, so this meant a long wall and a ticket office. There also had to be a waiting room, and bigger stations soon had separate rooms for men and women, with fires in winter, and a refreshment room selling food and drink. In Britain, stations had raised platforms level with the floors of the coaches, so the platform had to be as long as the trains. In most other countries passengers boarded from ground level, and so had to climb into the train up steps. Another feature of the busier stations was a roof covering most of the platform. The largest stations, in the big cities, had to handle so much traffic that they needed many platforms, and a large glass roof then had to be built over the whole area.

Above: *This porter worked for the Great Central Railway, probably at Marylebone Station, London, in 1907.*
Below, left: *Britain's newest main-line station is Birmingham International, built on the site of a previous station.*
Below: *Most stations, such as Lauda in West Germany, have platforms at rail level.*

Above: *In the old days even small stations had a large staff. On this platform in 1890, are eight railwaymen and two passengers.*

Many of these great stations still exist, giving us an insight into buildings that were completely new creations when they were designed over 100 years ago. But today the world's thousands of old stations are big problems. Some are simply not able to handle today's traffic, and it is not easy to rebuild a station. The biggest problem is that they were designed when labour was cheap, whereas today it costs fantastic amounts of money to keep on painting the old woodwork, repairing glass windows and heating the old waiting rooms. Wherever possible railways or cities are replacing old stations with new ones made of glass, concrete and aluminium. These need no looking after, for they have central heating and every kind of modern feature. The new stations look quite different and, like modern airports, are light and airy and speed the traveller from road or underground into his train, with a computer to check on seat reservations and a printer that stamps his ticket on a roll of blank card. But sometimes the townspeople dislike the idea of a new station because it would look so different. In some cases, such as Great Malvern in England, the old station is put on the special list of historic monuments that must be preserved, so the railway has to make do with its inefficiency and high costs. Many stations are on lines that have been closed, so now they have again become private houses.

TRAINS OF THE FUTURE

Just a few years ago many people were saying that railways might soon become obsolete. They did not think that trains could rival the convenience of the car or the speed of the jet. Trains, they thought, would simply become part of history. Today we know better. Though some lines have declined, the future of the world's railways has never before been so certain. Trains of the future will travel at speeds in excess of 300 kph over track like that in the view below of a modern German overhead electrified railway.

Aérotrain

The steel wheel running on a steel rail is such an efficient way of supporting a train (allowing high speed with very low resistance) that it seems senseless to do away with it. For very high speeds, however, there are advantages in supporting the train in some other way. One way is to use magnetic forces (which you can read about on pages 194 and 195). Technically, a slightly less difficult method is to use air cushions, very much like those which support air-cushion vehicles (hovercraft). The first research on the air-supported train was done in 1961-65 by the Bertin company in France. In 1965, a special company was formed to build full-size Aérotrains to prove the concept and if possible to start producing Aérotrain systems for use in France or elsewhere.

One of the drawbacks of the ordinary rail wheel at very high speeds is that it cannot transmit the tremendous power needed without slipping. Another is that the wheels and bogies are the heaviest parts of the train, while a third disadvantage is that it is difficult to make them ride the rails properly at speeds higher than 320

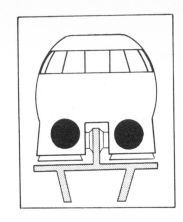

Above: *This drawing shows the front view of the Aérotrain 1-80. The car has a slit along the centre which guides it with air-cushion pads along the reinforced-concrete track. The other sketch shows the rear view of an earlier*

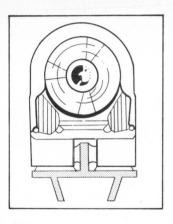

Aérotrain with propeller propulsion. **Below:** *Biggest of the Aérotrains so far run is the 1-80, or Orleans type, carrying 80 people at 426 kph. It has a turbofan engine on top, but is not very noisy.*

kph. Removing the wheels drastically reduces the weight and also cuts down air resistance at high speed. On the other hand, some of the power is consumed in pumping the air through the supporting cushions. The Bertin-type Aérotrain was planned around track shaped like a T upside-down. The supporting air cushions run along the flat track on each side, while guiding air cushions act on each side of a vertical central 'rail', like a narrow wall 550 millimetres high, fitting into a slot along the centre of the Aérotrain. Of course, at such high speeds single cars are more common than trains, but there is no reason why several should not be linked to form a train.

In operation, no part of the Aérotrain touches the track, unless it has to collect electric current by pick-ups. Those so far built have used their own power to drive the lift fans and **propulsion** (by air propellers or jet engines), except for the 44-seat urban Aérotrain for city use which had electric traction. Two test tracks were built, one at Gometz near Paris and the other just north of Orleans. Thousands of runs were made, often carrying passengers in sumptuous comfort at speeds up to 422 kph, but no public system has yet been constructed.

High-Speed Train

The High-Speed Train (HST) began service with British Rail in 1974. It will be the standard express passenger train on British non-electrified routes until the much more advanced APT (you can read about this on pages 186 and 187) is ready to enter service. There is little that is **revolutionary** about the HST though, like some earlier passenger trains, it has a 'power car' at each end which forms part of the train. The driver can sit at either end and control both power cars, so the train can run equally well in either direction.

A glance at the HST soon reveals how modern it looks. The power cars are streamlined and the coaches are of a completely new design, while the whole train is remarkably light in weight. The power cars, which are classed as diesel-electric locomotives of Class 41, each contain a Paxman Valenta diesel engine of 2,250 horse-power, and so are as powerful as many main-line diesels. But they are much shorter and lighter, and another change is the completely new cab with a central seat for the driver behind a large sloping window of unbreakable glass which looks like the windscreen of a jet. The cab controls are even newer in style than those of earlier diesels. Everything, in fact, has been scientifically designed to make it easier for the driver to work. The cab is completely **ventilated** and heated, and is rated the most comfortable cab in service.

The coaches are just the opposite in appearance: they are not short but long (22 metres), and they are air-conditioned and packed with new features such as disc brakes and automatic doors worked by tread mats. Like the power cars the new coaches are designed to cause less wear on the track, despite the fact that HST runs, even uphill, at speeds between 160 and 200 kph. The first HST set a diesel speed record of 230 kph on test in 1973. The following year it went into service on the British Western Region, and now many HSTs are in use on the Western and Eastern Regions, slashing journey times by about one-fifth whilst greatly improving comfort and passenger appeal. The HST is considered to be currently the best non-electrified train in the world.

Right: *Though faster than other trains, the HSTs are appreciated by the passengers for their great comfort. When this book was written the HST service speed was restricted to 200 kph, but they could run at about 230 kph if allowed. This is close to the limit with today's track.*

Right: *Other nations are also running High-Speed Trains. This streamliner runs on inter-city routes on the DB (German State Railways). Powered by electricity from an overhead wire, it has an exceptionally smooth exterior and very high power for its weight.*

Rapid Transit System

In the early 1960s one of the few big cities in the world to have no special 'rapid transit' system was San Francisco, in California. San Francisco is a very rich city and it could afford to build whatever it decided was the best system. It spent years studying the problem and planning where the new system would run. Among the kinds of transport system considered were monorails, tracked air-cushion vehicles (which you can read about on pages 192 and 193), magnetic-levitation vehicles (on pages 194 and 195), improved bus routes and various kinds of ordinary railway. Eventually, the choice fell on a railway, but one more advanced in **concept** than any other in the world. The new railway, which was built in 1968-72, is called the Bay Area Rapid Transit (BART).

Geographically, it is unlike any other **urban** rail system. Instead of serving just one city it links stations throughout San Francisco and its suburbs as well as the neighbouring urban centres on the east side of San Francisco Bay, such as Oakland, Alameda and Berkeley. The west and east parts are linked by twin tracks running through tunnels under the bay. These were built by lowering sections of tunnel to the sea-bed and then welding them in place. Altogether, there are 120 kilometres of double track, of which 40 kilometres are elevated above ground-level and much of the rest is underground. To improve safety and stability, it was decided to use a wider gauge than normal and the rails are 1.7 metres apart. Trains are thus broad, but low-slung, and their electric motors pick up current from the track and drive them at speeds up to 130 kph. Acceleration is very rapid, and braking is powerful and smooth.

Left: *San Francisco is extremely hilly. Here a BART train climbs steeply away from a station after having made a quick crossing of San Francisco Bay inside a tunnel. These light and powerful trains accelerate very quickly.*

Above: *This exciting scene shows a BART train zooming up from tracks laid along the centre of a ten-lane freeway (motorway). The new rapid-transit system was built to ease congestion on the overworked San Francisco highways. and is faster than cars.*

BART is the most automatic, computerized railway in the world. The whole system, which is extremely complicated, is controlled by vast computers and **supervized** by only two people on duty in a central control room. Each train does have a driver on board, but he normally has nothing to do but see that everything is running properly. Called an 'attendant', he sits behind a large front window, and could in emergency take over the driving of the train. The only trouble with BART is that it cost far more than was estimated, and it is proving impossible to run it at a profit.

Speeding on the Curves

While the HST is the best passenger train using today's technical knowledge, the Advanced Passenger Train (APT) is likely to be the best passenger train to use tomorrow's technology. In fact, it has been designed to be the ultimate train that can be designed to run over present track, though the route will need a few changes. For example, the spacing between signals will need to be adjusted in some places. But the whole idea of APT is that it uses today's railway, and does not need a new one such as the Tokaido Line. Like the HST, the APT is dramatically faster than today's trains, but this is only part of the story. It does not have to slow down so much on bends; for example, curves that would make an ordinary train slow to 80 kph are taken by APT at 120 kph and, because the coach bodies are smoothly tilted as the train runs round the curve, the passengers experience no discomfort. This is much more satisfactory than trains on some other railways where the coach bodies can swing from side to side like a pendulum; with APT the tilt is exactly controlled and there is no 'pendulum' swing. Another feature of APT is that it has fantastic

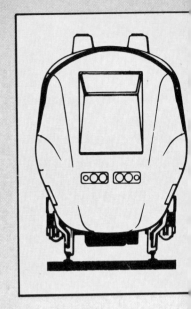

Above: *This front view of the APT shows the unusual cross-section shape. When the train comes to a bend the cars tilt (above, right).*

power for its weight, and so can **accelerate** very fast back to full speed.

The **prototype** APT began running in 1972. It was powered by ten 300-horsepower gas turbines—like miniature jet engines but geared to generators supplying current to electric traction motors driving the wheels. The gas turbines were about as big as car engines, and they were grouped about the floor of two five-engine power cars, one at each end of the train. This train, called APT-E (E for experimental), showed what it could do in August 1975 when it averaged 244 kph over a short stretch between Bristol and London. In October that year it ran from London to Leicester, 159 kilometres away, in 58 minutes, despite being forbidden to exceed 201 kph over almost the whole route.

In 1978, three production APTs are to go into use between London and Glasgow. This is an electrified route, so these trains will not need gas turbine engines but will have **pantographs** to draw current from the overhead wire like other electric trains. Each of these APTs will seat 614 passengers and be booked to cover the 645-kilometre journey in four hours. No other train could possibly do this.

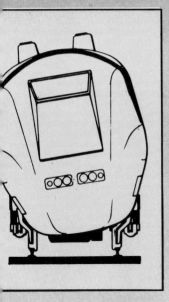

Below: APT-E looks rather like a Japanese Hikari train, but is actually quite different. It can go fast over ordinary tracks.

Riding on Air

TACV stands for 'tracked air-cushion vehicle'. In Britain ACVs are more popularly called hovercraft, and Britain once had a company called Tracked Hovercraft Ltd (THL) which spent many years in trying to build a TACV. It appeared to have the best and most advanced design in the world, but the government stopped it—mainly because of a decision by British Rail that it would never want to operate any track different from that now in use. In fact, the main fault of the TACV is that it does not fit today's rails, but that objection does not apply if a new route—for example, from a city to a new airport—has to be constructed anyway. The problems in trying to build a completely new kind of railway are not so much technical as financial. It costs so much money in the modern world that it is simpler never to do anything new at all.

The first TACV was actually the Aérotrain, but this was rather primitive and not very well designed. The THL Hovertrain began by constructing a better track, made from sections of reinforced concrete; it would be difficult to imagine a simpler or cheaper kind of track for any transport system, and it did not suffer from several drawbacks of the Aérotrain track (for example, the latter could be dangerously blocked by windblown snow, which is serious at 480 kph). The Hovertrain was lifted and guided by air-cushion pads made in two parts. A

Left: *A photograph of the Grumman vehicle on test at speed (up to 480 kph). With a length of 16 metres, this TACV provided much useful information. The Grumman scheme has side air cushions running along concrete walls in the guideway. It has down-facing cushions for lift, and also a slit along the centre for experiments with a central 'rail'.*

Above: *This TACV was built for the US Department of Transportation by an aerospace company, Grumman. At the back are three JT15D turbofans which provide propulsion and also blow air through the lift and side-guidance cushions.*

strongly-sprung portion took care of the big track changes (rise and fall across the landscape, or curves) while a weaker portion ironed out any small roughnesses in the concrete. This gave passengers a marvellously smooth ride. Propulsion or braking were by a linear induction motor (LIM), which is like an electric motor cut open and rolled out into a straight line. Electric coils on the train set up a **magnetic field** which reacted with an aluminium strip along the track to pull the train along, or, with current reversed, to slow it down.

TACV research has been slowed down in most countries, but after some 15 years of research in France and ten in the USA the prospects are better and there may soon be no technical problems to hold it back. The big difficulty is finding a completely new busy high-speed route where a simple and efficient TACV railway can be built and operated at attractive fares.

Running on Magnets

Maglev is a short way of writing 'magnetic levitation', which is a way of making something float simply by using magnets. It is even more difficult to make a Maglev train than to make a TACV, but if it can be done the result could be the best kind of railway yet. The basic idea is that the electric current supplied from the railway to the train should be used not only to propel it along but also to support it without requiring wheels to run on rails. But anyone who has ever played with magnets will see how difficult it is to turn the idea into a practical railway. Magnets tend to be difficult to control when they are close together. They repel each other and always want to whip around end-to-end and attract. So a Maglev car lifted by **repulsion** could always try to slide right off its track or turn round. Another problem is that, unless the magnet poles are very close together, the repulsion is not strong enough to lift the train.

There are several ways round these problems. One of the answers is not to lift by repulsion at all, but to arrange the magnets so that they lift the train by attraction. With clever design the Maglev car can be both lifted and guided by the same set of magnets, so that instead of the magnets tending to push it off the track they keep it running along the centre of the track, without any metal-to-metal contact. Another of the technical breakthroughs has been in the generation of the powerful magnetic field. There are two ways of generating a magnetic field to lift a train: one can use a permanent magnet, the other an electromagnet. The former is magnetized all the time, but it was only in the 1960s when engineers developed extremely powerful magnets pressed from 'ferrite' powder (a mixture of ceramics and ferric oxide) that permanent magnets could be made strong enough. The electromagnet works only when a current flows through a coil of wire around it. Thanks to a fantastic new kind of wire called a 'superconductor', which has an electrical resistance of virtually zero, electromagnets are now easily able to lift trains whilst consuming hardly any power. This makes the Maglev much less costly than the TACV.

The Germans are leading in the Maglev race, though money for research has had to be cut back. Krauss-Maffei, a well-known railway builder, is testing the Komet. By 1978 it is hoped to run a 160-seat Maglev at 500 kph. Such speeds would be of use only over quite long distances on new routes without bends.

194

Right: *A German Maglev car built, like the test vehicle above, by the Messerschmitt-Bölkow-Blohm company. Driven by a linear electric motor, it will lead to silent trains capable of a steady speed of at least 500 kph.*

Below: *This yellow-painted Maglev test vehicle is driven at fantastic speed by the battery of rockets shown behind it. It was the first full-size Maglev car built in Europe.*

Design for the Future

The only thing we can be sure of regarding the future of railways is that it will be exciting and go on for as far ahead as we can predict; but we cannot see clearly even to the end of the century. The basic fact is that railways are man's biggest worldwide network of fixed engineering equipment and this means that they cannot easily be changed. Even to alter the gauge of today's railway track would cost more than the world's nations could afford, and it will be a long time before we tear up the track completely and lay down something different over the same routes.

A rash of new ideas emerged in the late 1960s. One was a tracked ACV of giant size, intended for carrying freight. Each 'train' was to be a monster hovercraft about 20 metres wide, carrying hundreds of containers and equipped with a gantry to transfer these to trucks, ships or aircraft. The huge vehicle was to run at 320 kph over a broad concrete guideway. Another was a high-speed GVT (gravity-vacuum train) which would zoom down into the depths of the Earth in a tube, from which the air would be sucked to reduce resistance, and reaching about the speed of sound. Then the tube would rise gently back to the surface, slowing the GVT as it approached its destination.

Below: *Will this train ever run, sliding almost silently along a smooth ribbon of ice?*

Below: *An even more incredible scheme is the Gravity-Vacuum Train (GVT) plan, in which 'trains' would swoop through airless tunnels deep inside the Earth.*

STEAM LIVES ON

Everyone knows that some steam trains are preserved for fun, but in many countries steam trains still handle most or even all of the everyday traffic. In fact, in India big steam locomotives were still being built as recently as the late 1960s. Thousands of powerful 'steamers' are still hard at work in New Zealand, the Soviet Union, parts of Africa, South America, Australia and elsewhere. Probably all will soon be extinct, because steam locomotives are inefficient. Shown below is a preserved locomotive of the Great Western Railway.

Preserving the Past

All over the world interest in railways is so great that **enthusiasts** have formed clubs and societies specially to take care of old locomotives, rolling stock and many other items. Some working steam railways are miniatures, while many priceless items are in museums. But most rail enthusiasts would agree that it is best of all to preserve locomotives that actually work. This is not easy to do. To restore a steam locomotive to good condition can take months or even years of hard work. It then costs a lot of money to keep it running. If it is run only now and then, there is a severe risk of rusting and **corrosion** unless it is regularly cleaned in every nook and cranny. Fortunately, there is never a lack of willing helpers.

Many fine engines are preserved by clubs specially formed for the purpose, while other clubs—such as the A4 Locomotive Society—are concerned with particular classes of engines. Many locomotives are kept running at 'live museums' or 'steam centres' such as Steamtown in the north-east United States or Bressingham in Britain.

Above: *One of the most famous locomotives in the world, Flying Scotsman has been preserved in spotless running order.*

Below: *This narrow-gauge line in the Somme was built in the First World War to supply the front line. Today it has been restored as a tourist attraction.*

Many groups operate in partnership with the national railway. In several European countries, Western Australia and some US states the support comes at least partly from a tourist bureau, while in many cases it comes from private industry. One of the most famous engines of all, Flying Scotsman, was preserved and kept running by a single dedicated businessman, Alan Pegler.

Britain has more railway societies than any other country of similar size or population. Some are local, while others—notably the Locomotive Club of Great Britain—hold frequent meetings all over the country. Often a club will charter a special train for a planned outing, always organizing a preserved locomotive and if possible a special set of coaches, and paying a fee for permission to run over British Rail track and use signalling and other facilities. With a steam locomotive coal and soft water must be provided and a skilled driver who knows 'the road'.

Below: *Putting Pixie back on the rails in Leicestershire, England, where the vicar has a railway in his garden.*

Models and Miniatures

Railways had not been very long in existence before people started to make working model railways for pleasure. By 1850, toy trains were being made for children in factories, while super-detailed models were being constructed by adult enthusiasts, and the same is true today. In-between these models and full-size trains lie a wide range of miniature or narrow-gauge railways. All over the world there are miniature railways, typically with a gauge of about 150 millimetres, that carry small loads of people (mostly children) round a short loop of track. Most are electric, because that gives least trouble, but some use locomotives which run on small petrol engines. Very few make use of steam.

There are a much smaller number of miniature railways that are famous in their own right. Unlike the closed-loop sort, they cannot be packed up and taken to a fair or fête; they are as permanent and fixed as a full-size railway. One of the first and best-known is the Romney, Hythe & Dymchurch, which runs several kilometres along the English coast. In northern England is the Ravenglass & Eskdale, and there are many in France, Germany and other European countries. The largest number of all are probably in the United States, the best-known being the Hoot, Toot & Whistle Railroad near Chicago, which runs models of old-time steam trains.

Above: *A superb model of a 'Stirling eight-footer' in London's Science Museum.*
Left: *'Branston Junction' is a fine example of a landscaped model railway.*
Far Left: *Jason, a model Beyer-Garratt, worked in Dorset until 1965 carrying visitors and farm feedstuffs.*

Of course many full-size railways were built to a gauge much smaller than usual, either because there was no need to carry heavy loads or because the route was hilly and winding and could not carry big high-speed trains. Most of the mountain rack routes are of this type, and so are some quite extensive railways on level track. Many countries also have a growing number of preserved lines which, though built as serious transport routes, are now kept open for fun, and these are operated by miniature trains even if they have the standard gauge between the rails. Britain has the Bluebell Line, the Dart Valley, the Keighley and Worth Valley, the Severn Valley and several miniature lines in Wales.

203

Railway Relics

Today, millions of people around the world possess objects and relics that they have purchased—often at a high price—simply because they were once part of a working railway. As recently as 20 years ago, the collection of railway antiques was not at all a common pastime, and thousands of things were thrown on the scrap-heap that would today fetch immense sums if only they were still in existence. The fantastic growth in the cult of railway **memorabilia** is due to several factors. One is the immense popular appeal of railways and especially the old steam railways. Another is the replacement of steam traction by quite different forms of motive power. Another is the wish of an increasing number of people to combine their interest with the possession of objects which they expect will increase in value as the years go by. Yet another reason is that railway enthusiasts today are far better organized than ever before, so that each can be readily informed of what is going on; and, to meet their needs, there has grown up an industry to serve them.

Above: *A commemorative mug of the 1840s.*

Right: *This patented luncheon basket enabled travellers to brew tea as well as eat en route.*
Left: *A painting of the Royal Albert bridge at Saltash.*

Below: *A poster advertising the Golden Arrow express with Pullman coaches linking London and Paris.*

This railway-enthusiast industry begins with the railways themselves. Today, when a station is to be rebuilt, a locomotive withdrawn or a branch line closed, the railway will do its best to sell everything it can for the best price it can obtain. Old notices, fire buckets, hand-lamps, clocks and even a whole signal post may come under the **auctioneer's** hammer. Few people collect old road kerbstones or pavements, but many enthusiasts have bought old sleepers (ties) and other portions of track. But the best prices are paid for nameplates or number-plates from scrapped engines and for similar scarce and attractive items.

The railway-enthusiast industry sells many other items. Among them are old railway maps and modern copies; records of the sounds of locomotives long since vanished; old railway photographs and prints; and fine modern paintings showing scenes that often were never recorded at the time. Perhaps the biggest business of all is in the production of books and magazines. Enthusiasts will pay far more for an old time-table than they will for a present-day one!

Temple for Trains

We are fortunate that many of the earliest and most famous of all railway locomotives are still in existence—though almost all have been rebuilt more than once, and some are said to contain not one part of the original. Most of these priceless **relics** are in museums. The Rocket, perhaps the most famous engine in the world, is in the London Science Museum along with many other railway exhibits, but Locomotion, the even older engine that hauled the world's first passenger train on the Stockton & Darlington, is on view on the platform at Darlington Station. Most large British cities have museums devoted to science or transport, but the biggest railway museums are run by British Rail at York and Swindon. London has a Museum of British Transport at Clapham, but most of its larger railway exhibits have been moved to York.

Reputedly the largest transport museum in Europe is the Swiss Transport Museum at Lucerne. Other famous transport museums are in Munich, Berlin, Paris, Madrid and many other cities. In the United States the leading museum of technology is the Smithsonian Institution in Washington. Railroad museums are numerous, with major ones at Worthington (Ohio), Golden (Colorado) and Jackson (Tennessee); Steamtown, in New Hampshire is a 'working museum', and among the transport museums pride of place must be given to the one in St Louis and the Henry Ford Museum at Dearborn (Michigan).

All these museums are open to the public throughout the year, and sell detailed catalogues, photographs and railway literature. There is every hope that our great **heritage** of early railway locomotives, rolling stock and equipment will be preserved indefinitely, to provide a link with our railways of today.

Below: *Lucerne (Luzern), in Switzerland, has a large transport museum. This is the rail section.*

Below: *Lion is probably the oldest locomotive to have worked in recent years. Built in 1838 for goods traffic on the Liverpool & Manchester, she pulled trains in 1953 for a film ('The Titfield Thunderbolt') and never broke down. She was continually at work as a pumping engine for 70 years, but is now in the Science Museum.*

Right: *North Star was one of the great engines of the early Great Western. She hauled the first train out of London on 4 June 1838, and ran in express service for 33 years. By 1906 she was on the scrap-heap, but she was rescued and, with some parts reconstructed, is today on view in the Swindon museum, England.*

World Map

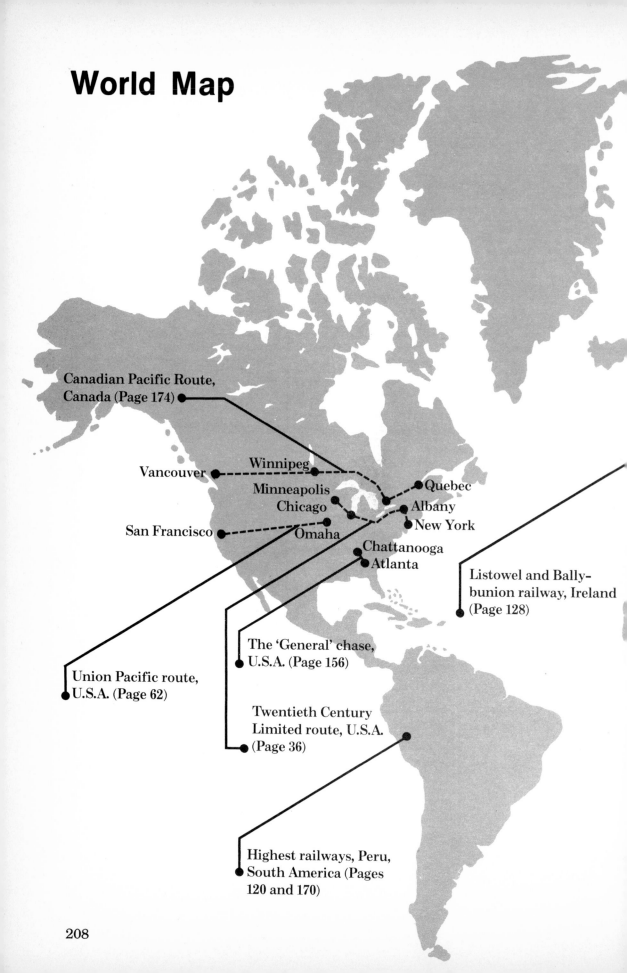

Canadian Pacific Route, Canada (Page 174)

Vancouver

Winnipeg

Minneapolis

Chicago

San Francisco

Omaha

Quebec

Albany

New York

Chattanooga

Atlanta

Listowel and Bally-bunion railway, Ireland (Page 128)

The 'General' chase, U.S.A. (Page 156)

Union Pacific route, U.S.A. (Page 62)

Twentieth Century Limited route, U.S.A. (Page 36)

Highest railways, Peru, South America (Pages 120 and 170)

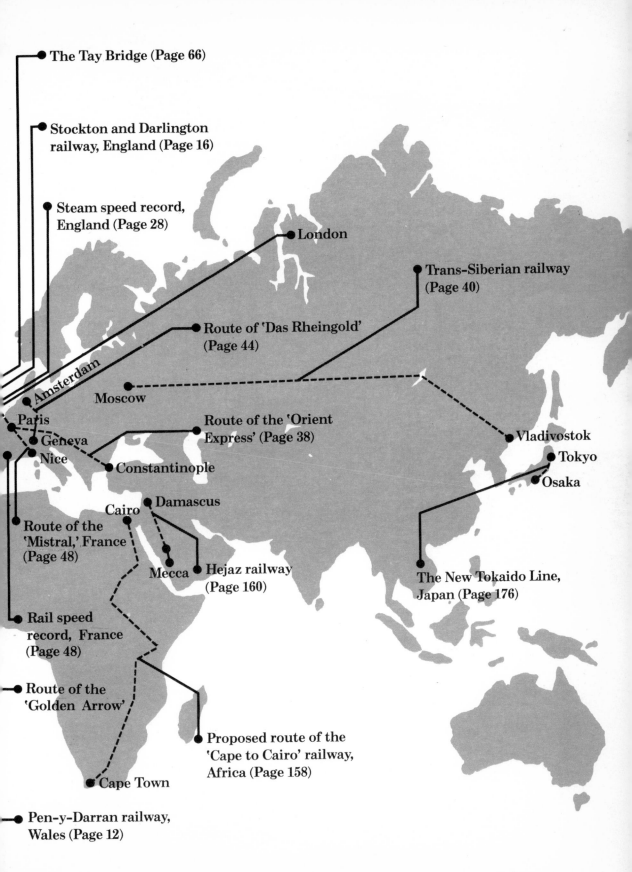

The Tay Bridge (Page 66)

Stockton and Darlington railway, England (Page 16)

Steam speed record, England (Page 28)

London

Trans-Siberian railway (Page 40)

Route of 'Das Rheingold' (Page 44)

Amsterdam

Moscow

Paris

Geneva

Nice

Route of the 'Orient Express' (Page 38)

Vladivostok

Tokyo

Osaka

Constantinople

Damascus

Cairo

Route of the 'Mistral,' France (Page 48)

Mecca

Hejaz railway (Page 160)

The New Tokaido Line, Japan (Page 176)

Rail speed record, France (Page 48)

Route of the 'Golden Arrow'

Proposed route of the 'Cape to Cairo' railway, Africa (Page 158)

Cape Town

Pen-y-Darran railway, Wales (Page 12)

Illustrated Glossary

A

Accelerate To increase speed. If a car or a train accelerates, it means that it goes faster and faster.

Adjacent Near to or bordering. If an article is adjacent to another, it means that the two are side by side or next to each other but not necessarily touching each other.

Advertisement The means by which information is made known to the public. For example, if a company wants people to know about its products, it may advertise them on a poster in a train or at a railway station. It may also endeavour to advertise them in newspapers, magazines or on television or commercial radio.

Alloy Two or more metals mixed together. Solder is an alloy of tin and lead; so too is pewter.

Architect A person who designs a building and then supervises the construction according to the plans.

Array To prepare or put in order for a purpose such as a special occasion.

Articulated Connected by a joint. An articulated trailer can be attached to a lorry and taken to a large railway station. There it can be detached from the lorry and put on to a train (below).

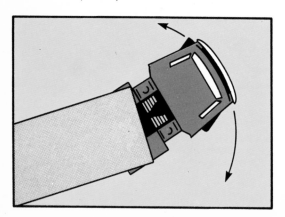

Atmospheric Pertaining to the Earth's atmosphere, i.e. the layer of gases like oxygen and nitrogen around the Earth. Atmospheric pressure is the pressure the atmosphere exerts on the Earth's surface.

Auctioneer The person who conducts an auction, a sale in which goods are sold in front of a group of interested people. The person who bids the highest amount succeeds in buying the article for sale.

Avalanche A mass of snow which moves with great force down the side of a mountain. An avalanche can also occur when rocks and earth slide down a mountain or a steep incline.

Axle A strong bar to which two wheels of a carriage or car are attached. The axle goes across the width of the vehicle and wheels are attached to either end through a hole in the centre, thus leaving the wheels free to turn around (below).

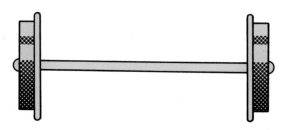

B

Ballast Heavy materials such as sand or cement or gravel used to form the bed of a railroad. Ships also have ballast to give them greater stability and to stop them rolling sideways.

Barricade A barrier or obstruction often used as a defence to stop someone going in or out of a place.

C

Calibre The internal diameter of any tube or cylinder made of metal (below).

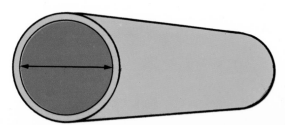

Canopy A raised covering placed over a seat or a doorway forming a sort of roof.

Chaldron An old measure of coal which held about 1,270 litres.

Chassis The chassis of a train or car is the framework upon which is mounted the body, the engine and the other working parts.

Commence To begin or to start.

Commodity An article of saleable or real value. Minerals and foodstuffs are commodities because people need them and are willing to pay for them.

Communications Systems by which information can be relayed or imparted from one person or place to another. Railways formed an important early communications system.

Commuter A person who travels a considerable distance from his home to his place of work is called a commuter. Most large cities have commuter areas, suburbs or towns out of the central area which are linked either by rail or by road.

Compressed To force something so that it will fit into a smaller space. A sponge is a good example of something that can be compressed. When air is compressed it becomes very hot so that if fuel is added it ignites quickly *(below)*.

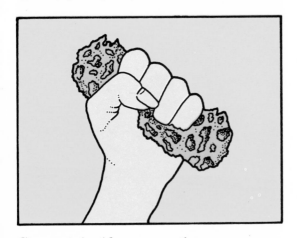

Concept An idea or a notion.

Congestion Too many things crowded into a limited space. A city is congested when too many people live in it. A road is congested when too many cars are driven on it.

Continental Pertaining to a continent, a very large mass of land. In Britain, a continental train is one which is going to Europe.

Corrosion A chemical action which slowly eats away at something and damages it. Trains, cars and steel boats all suffer corrosion when rust eats into their metal parts.

Cow catcher A steel grated shield at the front of a locomotive which pushes out of the way anything on the railway track *(below)*.

Customs officer A man who supervises the goods coming into a country. Some goods are not allowed in at all, others are allowed in if a tax is paid on them.

Cylinder A tube. A cylinder is long and straight and stretches between two circles at either end.

D

Deflector An instrument which causes something to be turned away or aside.

Detour An alternative way around an obstacle. If a road or a railway line is blocked, it is necessary to detour or to find another way around the obstacle.

Diameter A straight line drawn through the centre of a circle and touching its circumference at either side.

Diesel An internal combustion engine that burns heavy oil which is ignited by the compression of air. The oil it burns is also called diesel.

Diplomat A man skilled in the tactful handling of difficult situations or people. The term is used particularly to apply to the people who handle international affairs.

E

Effort An attempt to do something. If you really try hard to pass an exam, you are making an effort. A train employs a tremendous amount of mechanical effort to climb a hill for example.

Electrification To change from one form of power to electricity. When railways changed from steam or diesel to electricity-operated trains, the change was called electrification.

Electrified To charge something with electricity; to pass an electric current through something.

Embellished To elaborate or to add extra details to a story or an object. In the 19th century engines of several railway companies were embellished to give them a more striking appearance.

Engineer A man who has been trained in a practical science, usually to do with machines. A locomotive engineer spends many years learning all about the engine, how it works and how to fix it when something goes wrong.

Engineering The science concerned with the principles underlying the design, construction and use of engines.

Enginewright A man who used to be in charge of machines and engines used in an industry.

Enterprise A person who shows imagination or originality in an undertaking is said to have shown enterprise. As a noun, enterprise is the undertaking itself. Private enterprise means private companies or individuals in business as opposed to public companies supervised by governments.

Enthusiast Someone who follows a hobby or cause with great keenness and energy.

Environment Our surroundings, the things around us.

Escalator A moving staircase which works on a continuous chain. While you stand still, the escalator takes you up or down. If an escalator breaks down, it can still be used as an ordinary staircase. There are also travalators which are moving walkways.

Estuary The tidal mouth of a river which is usually quite wide. The estuary is where the river enters the sea *(below)*.

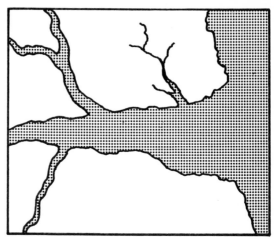

Exhaust The waste gases of an engine which are usually channelled out through a pipe running from the engine to the back.

Expand To enlarge or to grow bigger.

Expanded Enlarged.

F

Facility Something which makes life easier is called a facility. It could be something built for a special purpose. At a railway station, we would call a snack bar a facility: so are lavatories and washbasins.

Financial tycoon A person who deals with large amounts of money and who invests it to make greater profits. He is a man with a keen sense of business.

Flexible Something which can be bent easily without breaking. Rubber is flexible; cast iron is not. A person is described as flexible if he is able to adapt to situations.

Foundations The support that is built at the base of a structure.

Frame The structure which reinforces and gives shape to a machine or building. It is designed to both surround and support something.

Freight All sorts of products and materials carried from one place to another. A train which is especially designed to transport goods is called a freight train.

G

Gantry crane A travelling crane which is mounted on a platform and supported by side frames *(below)*.

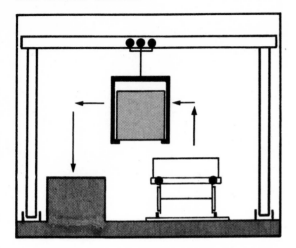

Gauge An instrument with a dial which indicates the quantity of something such as water, petrol or diesel. Gauge is also used to indicate the distance between rails on a railway track.

Gearbox A box containing different gears which allows a vehicle the speed or power it needs in different conditions. If a train is going up a hill, it needs extra power so a low gear is used: when it is on a clear, straight stretch of track, a high gear allows it to go more quickly.

Generator A machine which converts mechanical energy into electrical energy or for producing gas or steam.

Gradient The degree of a slope.

Grate area A frame of metal bars used in a fireplace for holding solid fuel such as coal or wood.

H

Headlamp A light at the front of a vehicle which is used at night time to light the track ahead and enables the driver to see where he is going.

Heritage What is passed down from one generation to the next. It can mean characteristics we inherit from our parents or it can mean the traditions and history of our school, culture or country.

Horizontal A line that is parallel to the horizon. This means the line must be flat or level. The top of a bookcase is horizontal.

Horsepower A unit of power. The term took its name from the amount of work one horse could do if it was pulling a weight.

I

Ignition A device for igniting or exploding a mixture of gases by an electric spark, used in engines *(below)*.

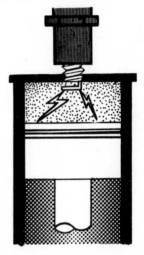

Illuminated Lit up.

Inclined To lean or slope away from the vertical or horizontal. Several steam engines of the 19th century had inclined cylinders.

Inhabited To be lived in. A town is inhabited when a number of people live there.

Insignia A badge or an emblem. People wear insignias to denote a rank or a particular honour *(below)*.

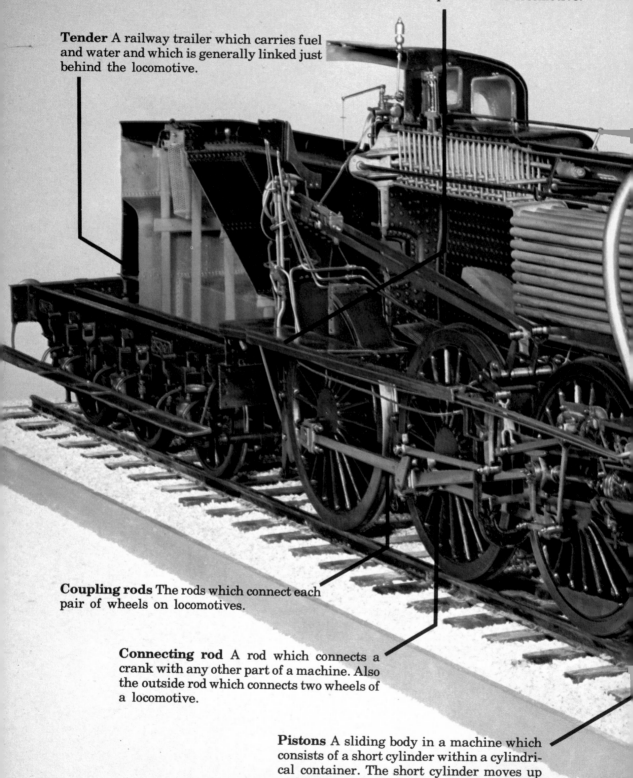

Footplate The floor or platform of a locomotive which enables the driver and crew to reach various parts of the locomotive.

Tender A railway trailer which carries fuel and water and which is generally linked just behind the locomotive.

Coupling rods The rods which connect each pair of wheels on locomotives.

Connecting rod A rod which connects a crank with any other part of a machine. Also the outside rod which connects two wheels of a locomotive.

Pistons A sliding body in a machine which consists of a short cylinder within a cylindrical container. The short cylinder moves up and down with the pressure of the engine.

214

Bogie A carriage whose frame has one or two pairs of wheels pivoted below the frame of a railway carriage or locomotive.

Smokestack The funnel of a steam locomotive which allows smoke to escape out of the fire box. It is also common on steamships.

Coupling Metal links which join the carriages together or a carriage to the engine.

Insulated When one thing is kept apart from another, it is insulated. Electric wires are insulated by a tube of rubber to keep the wires away from things on the outside. Containers for food can be insulated so the food inside can be kept cool and fresh. Houses can also be insulated against the cold outside *(below)*.

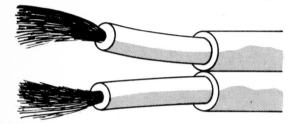

Interval A period of time between two events. At the theatre, the different acts of a play are separated from each other by a number of intervals.

L

Legendary Pertaining to a legend, a famous story of the past which may or may not be true.

Luxurious If we said someone lived in luxurious surroundings, we would mean they lived with rich and pleasing things around them.

M

Magnetic field The area in which a magnet exerts its influence. A magnet is a mass of iron which either attracts or repels other masses of iron *(below)*.

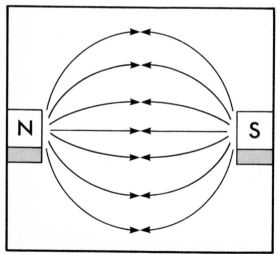

Marshalling yard Sidings where carriages and locomotives can be parked or moved around. Carriages can be disconnected from each other and joined together in a different order and on to a different locomotive.

Memorabilia Articles from the past which have nostalgic value or are worthy of being retained.

Monorail Literally, it means one rail. There are two types of monorails—one is suspended from an overhead rail, the other sits on a rail on the ground. Side wheels are needed on both types to keep the train steady *(below)*.

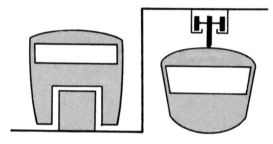

Munitions Weapons needed for war such as guns, rifles, bullets and shells.

N

Network An organized system of lines or channels fulfilling a specific purpose.

O

Ornamental Decorative. Something which does not serve a practical purpose but beautifies an object or person.

P

Pantographs The apparatus mounted on the top of electric trains for picking up the electric power from overhead wires *(below)*.

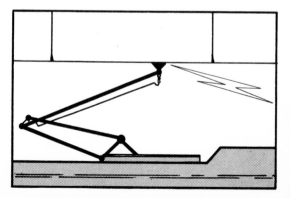

Pegs Wooden or metal pins which are usually tapered and which are used to fasten a frame together.

Pinions Small cogwheels which have teeth or grooves which mesh with the teeth of a larger cogwheel *(below)*.

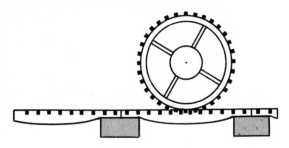

Pivot A fixed point on which something turns or revolves.

Pollution Matter which makes other things dirty. Steam from trains polluted the countryside, fumes from motor cars now pollute the cities, man's waste products from factories pollute rivers and lakes.

Propeller Blades which steer or drive an object forwards such as the propellers on boats and planes.

Propulsion Something that forces a vehicle to go forwards.

Prototype A model or pattern on which others are based. It is usually the first full-scale form of a new type or design of a construction.

Q
Quarters The lodgings used by gangs of navvies in the town through which the railway line was then passing.

R
Radical Something new or extreme. An idea which is very different from anything that went before it.

Realign To align again; to reorganize or make new groupings of things which were previously organized differently.

Regulator A machine which controls, or regulates, the quantity of something.

Relic A memento of the past.

Repulsion The act of driving back or rejecting.

Revenue The money which comes in to a person, a company or a country is known as revenue.

Reverse To make something go backwards. Most vehicles, like locomotives and cars, have a reverse gear which enables the vehicle to move backwards instead of forwards.

Revolution A complete change in a situation. The invention of the locomotive was a revolution because it completely changed means of transport. If the term is applied to a country, such as the Russian revolution, it means an uprising, usually violent, has led to a complete change in the ruling group of that country.

Rival A competitor. We say that two people are rivals when they are both competing for the same job.

Rivet A short bolt used to hold metal plates together. Its headless end is pressed down after passing through two holes *(below)*.

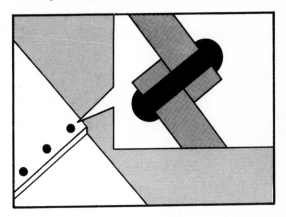

Rotary A rotary machine turns around in regular circles on an axis.

S
Safety valve A device which allows excess pressure in a boiler or hydraulic machine to escape so that the machine does not explode.

Schedule A time-table. Railway services try to keep to a schedule to arrive and depart from a station at a particular time. This enables passengers to know when they can catch their train to any destination.

Shaft A shaft means a stem, or a long, straight object. When it is applied to mining, it means the entrance, which is either long and straight or slightly inclined, penetrating into the mine.

Shareholder A person who owns part, or a share, of a company. A shareholder has shares or certificates which prove his part ownership. Some companies issue a large number of shares; others only a few. The shareholder shares in the profits of the company.

Sleeper Blocks on which the steel railway tracks stand. They may be made of steel, wood or concrete and they keep the tracks raised slightly off the ground *(below)*.

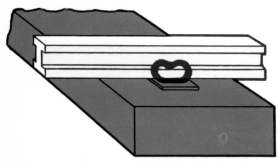

Spiralling Something which winds upwards continually, curving around a centre.

Spoil To impair or do harm to. To spoil something means to make it less pleasant than it was.

Spoke Any one of the bars connecting the hub of a wheel with the outer rim *(below)*.

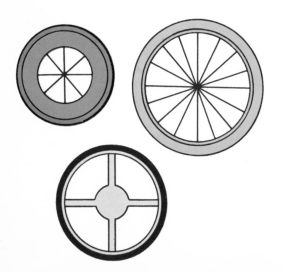

Straddle To bestride or to stand or walk with legs wide apart. A monorail is said to straddle a bar because appendages hang down on either side of the bar.

Stationary At a stop, not moving. A train is stationary when it has stopped at a siding or at a station.

Suburb The areas on the outskirts of a town or city which are predominantly residential.

Sulphurous Containing sulphur, a non-metallic element used in such things as matches and fireworks.

Superstitious Someone who believes in magic or supernatural occurrences is described as being superstitious.

Superstructure The ties, rails and fastenings of a railroad track.

Supervise To oversee or to superintend. Someone who checks on the work of others and the quality of goods produced supervises that work.

Surveyor A person who measures and records the exact nature, shape and features of a piece of land *(below)*.

Suspended Something which hangs from above is suspended. Lamps are suspended from a ceiling. One type of monorail is suspended from a rail which is fixed well above the ground.

Swivelling A ring and pivot which connects two parts and allows one to revolve around the other. A common example is a swivel chair which can swing around in circles without the central base moving.

T

Tandem Two people or objects, one behind the other. Horses harnessed one behind the other are in tandem. A bicycle with one seat behind the other is called a tandem *(below)*.

Technology The science of mechanical and industrial skills and knowledge.

Toll A payment which is made for the right to use a road or bridge by the vehicle using it. Tolls have often been used to pay for the construction of a new bridge.

Traction The act of pulling along. A traction engine was a moveable steam engine used to pull a heavy load.

Transfer To move from one place to another. You may transfer a cup from a table to a sideboard; or you may transfer from one train to another.

Turbine A rotating wheel driven by jets of water or steam which is used as the prime mover to work something else *(below)*.

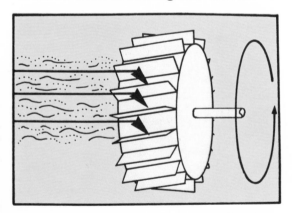

U

Urban Relating to a town or a city. An urban environment is one in which the surroundings are those of office blocks, flats and other buildings in close proximity to each other.

V

Ventilate To circulate fresh air around an enclosed area.

Vertical Up and down. A line that is at right angles to the ground is vertical. A lamp post, for example, is vertical.

Vistadome A special carriage fitted with big glass windows and a glass top in which passengers get a clear view of the countryside through which the train is passing.

W

Wedge A solid piece of material sharpened into a triangle at one end and wide at the other. It can be used as a lever to shift a heavy object *(below)*.

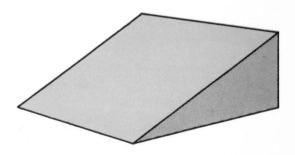

Weld Joining metal together. Welding can be done by heating the metal and hammering it or by applying molten metal, called solder, to the surfaces of the metal to be joined *(below)*.

Index

Where figures are in bold type this shows that they refer to illustrations or photographs

---